The Reader's Digest

QUIZ BOOK

The Reader's Digest

WORD POWER QUIZ BOOK

1,000 word challenges from
the world's most widely
read magazine

Reader's Digest

THE READER'S DIGEST ASSOCIATION (CANADA) LTD.
Montreal   London   Sydney

Text design by Michele Italiano-Perla
Text illustration by Mike Quon Design

The credits that appear on page 216 are hereby made a part of this copyright page.

Published by The Reader's Digest Association (Canada) Ltd.
215 Redfern Avenue, Westmount, Quebec H3Z 2V9

Canadian Cataloguing in Publication Data
Main entry under title:
   The Reader's Digest word power quiz book

(Quips, quotes and quizzes)
Word power quizzes compiled from Reader's Digest
magazine dept., It pays to enrich your word power.
ISBN 0-88850-598-1 (set)-
ISBN 0-88850-595-7

1. Vocabulary—Problems, exercises, etc. I. Reader's Digest
Association (Canada). II. Title: Word power quiz book. III. Series.

PE1449.R43 1997   428.1   C97-900387-3

This book is based on an American concept produced by The Reader's Digest Association, Inc. All of the extracts have previously appeared in editions of the Reader's Digest magazine.

Words sing. They hurt. They teach. They sanctify.

They were man's first, immeasurable feat of magic.

They liberated us from ignorance and our barbarous past.

—*Leo Rosten*

eader's Digest has always been a magazine for people who seek to expand their horizons, to improve their abilities, to achieve their goals. No other feature exemplifies this better than "It Pays to Enrich Your Word Power". Over the years, it has come to be known as the department people turn to first, to diversify and enrich the words they use at home, in the classroom and in the workplace.

Today, everyone is looking for the secret to achieving successful language skills. New audiotapes, videos and computer programs come and go, promising quick fixes and short cuts to a better vocabulary.

But, for many years, *Reader's Digest* has had the secret. There have been no gimmicks, no clever packaging, no short cuts, no boring lectures: just "Word Power". One page of twenty words and eighty possible choices and another page of twenty answers. Seemingly so simple, yet so challenging.

If there is a key to the success of "Word Power", that's it: the challenge. Everyone strives for the department's "Exceptional" ranking. Some achieve it, others do not. But each month, everyone returns, ready to try again. Readers of *The Digest* know that with "Word Power" a mistake is never a set-back, it is simply another opportunity to learn.

The Editors

Overheard at an elementary school: "Now remember, class, if you don't learn penmanship, when you grow up you'll have to pay cash for everything."
—EDWARD T. GRANEY

"You will stay young as long as you learn, form new habits and don't mind being contradicted."
—MARIE VON EBNER-ESCHENBACH

Henry James, criticising a fellow novelist: "She began several years ago writing unmitigated nonsense, and now she writes nonsense very sensibly mitigated."

CONTENTS

M̲y friend Harry told me about a joke he'd played on his wife that demonstrates the power of a word.

"As company amanuensis, my wife, Mary, keeps the books at our company and answers most of the mail. During a recent holiday to Puerto Rico, my sense of humour soon led me into some wordplay. Anticipating that few in our group would know the definition of the word, I confided to some of the fellows in a low voice that I was on holiday with my amanuensis."

Harry laughed. "By the time the plane landed, Mary noticed, to her distress, that the women were avoiding her and the men looking at her with increased interest. I think they envied me and wished they dared to go off with an amanuensis. I was enjoying the joke so much, the ramifications didn't occur to me. Later Mary chatted with one of the wives about our eight grandchildren and our joy in them. The joke was over.

"When Mary realised what I'd done she was furious. 'And you didn't explain that an amanuensis is simply someone who writes letters and takes dictation?'

"I mollified her by saying that as a grandmother she should be proud to be taken for my amanuensis—whatever that word might have meant to those good people."

MY AFFLICTIVE SATURDAY MORNINGS:
The Origins of "Word Power"

My father, Wilfred Funk, would have relished this
story, for he knew well the power of words. Son of
Dr. I. K. Funk, a lexicographer who created Funk &
Wagnalls and the dictionary, he was a poet as well as
a lexicographer.

My father's initial inspiration for his books on
vocabulary-building and the *Reader's Digest* feature
"It Pays to Enrich Your Word Power" came from his
fuming about the way schools taught vocabulary.
When I brought home a list of words to memorise
with their definitions, he'd shake his head in disgust.
"What an asinine way to treat words. How could anyone learn to love words without knowing something
about them, how they're used or where they've come
from? It's a crime against our exquisite language."

Words held a magical wonder for him. They
represented the culmination of civilisation, each in
some way a repository of the past. He'd marvel at the
appearance of every new scientific term that might
quickly spawn a dozen other words. He described
words until they shimmered with the excitement
of life.

Even so, I dreaded Saturday mornings. My
brother, sisters and I became my father's vocabulary-
building guinea pigs, and every Saturday morning
after breakfast he would try out various vocabulary

tests on us. But this was Saturday! I had other things on my mind than taking tests. His enthusiasm, however, eventually ensnared me. I began to see words through my father's eyes and to become fascinated by what he called these Alice in Wonderland creatures.

Later he wrote the pioneering vocabulary-builder *30 Days to a More Powerful Vocabulary*. It became a bestseller and the prototype of the flood of vocabulary-builders that followed.

In 1944 he worked up a word quiz with an inspiring introduction and took it to DeWitt Wallace, founder and editor-in-chief of *Reader's Digest*. With keen editorial insight Mr. Wallace foresaw the phenomenal popularity it would have among *Reader's Digest* readers, not only in the United States but around the world. The feature appeared in the January 1945 issue. I've written it since 1965.

David Crystal, an English lecturer, writer and broadcaster on linguistics, said of "Word Power" that "the world-famous page from *Reader's Digest* has persuaded several generations of readers to take an interest in their vocabulary."

INCREASING WORD POWER
DEVELOPS BRAIN POWER

My many years as a lexical semanticist (a scholar who studies the meaning of words) have led me to adapt Wittgenstein's observation to my own experience: The limits of the size and quality of our vocabulary form the limits of our minds. And I especially stress quality over sheer size.

For example, concept words are quality words having to do with ideas. They stimulate us to think in new ways. *Integrity* is a concept word, as are *heuristic*, *reify*, *entropy*, *revelation*, *coalesce*, *dissident* and *compassion*. All of these words are found in the various tests in this book.

Whenever we learn a new word, it is not just dumped into our "mental dictionary". Our brain creates neuron connections between the new word and others relevant to our interests. It develops new perceptions and concepts.

HOW LARGE IS LARGE?

What is the size of your vocabulary? It has been estimated that a secondary school graduate may know up to 25,000 words, a college graduate up to 50,000. Yet our actual vocabularies are difficult to assess. Take the words *run*, *running* and *ran*. Are *running* and *ran* simply different forms of *run*? Or do they constitute a vocabulary of three words? Today most lexical semanticists choose to count only the basic form of the word.

According to David Crystal in *The Cambridge Encyclopaedia of the English Language* "[the size of one's vocabulary] depends on a person's hobbies and educational background. Someone who reads several novels a week is obviously going to pick up a larger vocabulary than someone whose daily reading is restricted to the telephone directory. And a degree in chemistry or botany will result in an enormous increase in (a specialised) vocabulary." Such a scientific vocabulary, however, is not of much use in ordinary communication.

From my work on "It Pays to Enrich Your Word Power", I estimate that, eliminating highly technical words employed by relatively few people, the essential English language we use to communicate with each other consists of about 15,000 words.

GETTING TO KNOW YOU

I find it frustrating to learn a new word and then, when it's just the one I need, to be unable to recall it. Here are a few helpful tips.

Make flash cards on which to write new words, with illustrations of their usage. Include origins, for they can be an aid to remembering a word. Add one or two of the closest synonyms from the thesaurus to gain a sense of the word's range.

For the first week or so, use these words as often as possible in your speaking and writing.

Get the best dictionary. If you can afford it, buy two: a desk or concise edition and an unabridged one, both in the most recent versions available. You need the latest guide to our ever-changing language.

Another volume to have is a thesaurus. English, more than any other language, has vast numbers of synonyms. A synonym gives a slightly different slant to the meaning of a word, adding precision to your thinking and communicating. A synonym is to a writer or speaker what a shade of colour is to a painter.

WHAT "WORD POWER" WILL DO FOR YOU

Brain experts claim that your ability to learn can remain steady throughout your life. And what do they point to as one of the surest and most enjoyable ways to expand your brain power? Enriching your word power. These quizzes will be a powerful aid in this endeavour.

• You will learn many new words. You will also refresh your memory of those words that you know but haven't used for a while.

• You will discover how certain words relate to the lives and thoughts of famous personalities.

• You will read about the fascinating etymologies that add so much to word lore.

• You will find a host of words that are relative newcomers to the English language. The English language has never been on a leash. It has roamed freely, returning home with "friends" from all over the world, from science, technology, various ethnic groups and other nations and cultures.

Most of all, our hope is that you will find a new enthusiasm for adding to your "word power" and that this book will bring greater richness and pleasure to your life.

Peter Funk

"In the beginning was the word." Logos, *the Greek term originally used for "word" in this Bible verse from the New Testament, and its Latin counterpart* loqui, *have given birth to numerous words. Each word in this quiz derives from one or the other. Select the answer you think is correct. Turn the page for your score.*

ventriloquism — A: repetition of words. B: method of recording. C: "throwing" one's voice. D: speech impairment.

loquacious — A: evasive. B: multilingual. C: unctuous. D: talkative.

monologue — A: long speech. B: scholarly work. C: editorial. D: hum.

terminology — A: nomenclature. B: extremity. C: mannerism. D: grammar.

elocution — A: deprecation. B: oratory. C: appeal. D: legalese.

interlocutor — A: go-between. B: researcher. C: dialogist. D: translator.

tautology — A: consistency in reasoning. B: careful instruction. C: nervousness. D: unnecessary repetition.

eulogy — A: formal praise. B: graduation speech. C: promise. D: sorrowful poem.

apologist — someone who A: broods on the past. B: makes no excuses. C: is fearful. D: defends an idea.

prologue — A: introduction. B: explication. C: game plan. D: précis.

❝Speak the truth, but leave immediately after.**❞**

—SLOVENIAN PROVERB

"Talking is like playing the harp; there is as much in laying the hands on the strings to stop their vibrations as in twanging them to bring out their music.**"**

—*OLIVER WENDELL HOLMES, SR.*

---

philology — study of A: basic truths. B: races and cultures. C: nonverbal language. D: literary texts.

Decalogue — A: famous series of plays. B: Ten Commandments. C: type of exile. D: permanent record.

lexicologist — one who A: announces sports. B: trains birds to speak. C: writes letters. D: studies word meanings and origins.

analogy — A: detailed examination. B: partial similarity. C: newly coined word. D: figure of speech.

logophile — lover of A: words. B: books. C: trademarks. D: sermons.

dialogue — A: argument. B: instruction. C: conversation. D: lecture.

circumlocution — A: faux pas. B: search. C: innuendo. D: verbosity.

sinologist — expert in A: origins of evil. B: Chinese civilisation. C: sign language. D: head colds.

cosmology — study of A: the universe. B: plastic surgery. C: city life. D: earth's surface.

epilogue — A: comedy. B: plot line. C: concluding statement. D: beginning of a story.

 *ANSWERS*

ventriloquism — C: "Throwing" one's voice; Latin *ventriloquus* (one who speaks from the belly).

loquacious — D: A mildly disparaging term for being talkative or wordy; as, a *loquacious* salesman. Latin *loqui* (to speak).

monologue — A: Long speech by a single speaker, monopolizing a conversation; dramatic speech by one actor. Greek *monologos* (speaking alone).

terminology — A: Nomenclature; technical terms relating to a specific subject. Latin *terminus* (limit) and Greek *logos* (word, speech).

elocution — B: Oratory; style or manner of speaking or reading in public. Latin *eloqui* (to speak out).

interlocutor — C: Dialogist; person who takes part in a conversation or discussion and who may ask questions; as, The journalist was a skilled *interlocutor*. Latin *interloqui* (to speak between).

tautology — D: Unnecessary repetition of an idea in different words. Greek *tauto* (the same) and *logos*.

eulogy — A: Formal praise of a person, especially one who has died recently. Greek *eulogia* (praise).

apologist — D: One who explains or defends an idea, cause or person; as, an *apologist* for tough laws against drug dealers. Greek *apologia* (speech in defence).

prologue — A: Introduction to a poem, play, book, etc.; preliminary event; as, The conference of American and Russian negotiators was a *prologue* to a summit meeting. Greek *pro-* (for) and *logos*.

philology — D: Study of literary texts and written records to determine their authenticity and meaning. Greek *philein* (to love) and *logos*.

Decalogue — B: The Ten Commandments. Greek *deka* (ten) and *logos*.

lexicologist — D: One who studies the formation of words and their derivations, meanings and uses. Greek *lexikos* (of words) and *logos*.

analogy — B: Partial similarity of things unlike in various aspects but forming a basis for comparison; as, the *analogy* of a human lung to a balloon. Greek *ana* (similar to) and *logos*.

logophile — A: Lover of words; as, Many of you who read this feature are *logophiles*. Greek *logos* and *philos* (loving).

dialogue — C: Conversation; especially a frank exchange of different points of view. Greek *dialogos*.

circumlocution — D: Verbosity; roundabout way of speaking or writing; as, Come to the point. Don't use *circumlocutions*. Latin *circum-* (around) and *loqui*.

sinologist — B: An expert in Chinese language, literature, history, art and customs. Greek *Sinai* (the Chinese people) and *logos*.

cosmology — A: The study of the nature, origin, structure and evolution of the universe. Greek *kosmos* (universe) and *logos*.

epilogue — C: Concluding statement of a novel or play, giving further insight; as, the *epilogue* spoken by Prospero in Shakespeare's *The Tempest*. Greek *epilogos*.

Vocabulary Ratings
> 9 — 11 correct ... Good
> 12 — 17 correct ... Excellent
> 18 — 20 correct ... Exceptional

EUPHUNISMS
Cheap: fiscally retentive

Crooked: ethically challenged —Constance Brancato

Old: chronologically gifted
—George O. Ludcke in *The Wall Street Journal*

LATIN LIVES ON

Latin is enjoying a revival in many schools today. Since more than half of our English words derive from Latin, in a sense we speak it every day. Bring the following words and phrases to life. Turn the page to find your score.

nonplussed — A: displeased. B: diminished. C: dumbfounded. D: blocked.

terra firma — A: fright. B: determination. C: solid ground. D: indecision.

bona fide — A: with optimism. B: free. C: costly. D: in good faith.

nota bene — A: to act generously. B: note well. C: ignore. D: bless.

alter ego — A: foe. B: other self. C: honoured mentor. D: uncertainty.

in loco parentis — A: eccentric parents. B: in place of a parent. C: in a safe place. D: in quest of a place.

persona non grata — a person who is A: lacking in manners. B: unacceptable. C: not responsible. D: ungrateful.

caveat emptor — A: ignore hunger. B: let the buyer beware. C: first come, first served. D: never give up.

sub rosa — A: beautifully. B: carefully. C: secretly. D: colourfully.

per diem — A: over and over again. B: for the moment. C: gradually. D: by the day.

per se — A: as if. B: just the way it is. C: because. D: by or in itself.

❝If you have a garden and a library, you have everything you need.**❞**

—CICERO

" Fable is more historical than fact, because fact

tells us about one man and fable tells us

about a million men. **"**

—G. K. CHESTERTON

---

sine qua non — A: everything is gone. B: out of sight, out of mind.
C: without which there is nothing. D: mentally unsound.

et al. — A: altogether. B: the end. C: and others. D: there are no
leftovers.

ad nauseam — A: to a sickening degree. B: uncouth. C: evil.
D: foul-smelling.

in extremis — A: the nearest site. B: stretched to the limit.
C: at the point of death. D: disgraced.

in vitro — A: dipped in wine. B: fully alive. C: according to law.
D: artificially maintained.

modus operandi — A: way of working. B: big-time operator.
C: sense of the future. D: international agreement.

ex officio — A: formerly. B: out of office. C: unofficially.
D: by virtue of office.

quid pro quo — A: something for nothing. B: easy come, easy go.
C: in payment of. D: something for something.

status quo — A: existing condition. B: precedent. C: sum total.
D: decree.

" A different language is a different vision of life. **"**

—FEDERICO FELLINI, QUOTED BY MARY CANTWELL IN THE NEW YORK TIMES

nonplussed — C: Dumbfounded. When *nonplussed*, we are so stunned that we temporarily can't act or think. *Non-* (not) and *plus* (more).

terra firma — C: Solid ground; as, Back on the dock, the seasick passenger said, "Am I glad to be on *terra firma!*"

bona fide — D: In good faith; sincere; genuine; as, He made a *bona fide* offer for the beach cottage.

nota bene — B: Note well or observe. Usually abbreviated as *N.B.* and used to call attention to something; as, *N.B.* Appointment of this judge will have a lasting effect.

alter ego — B: Other self; perfect substitute; intimate friend; as, Her husband became her *alter ego*.

in loco parentis — B: In the place or role of a parent; as, The university stated it would not act *in loco parentis* for the student.

persona non grata — B: A person unacceptable or not welcome; as, The attaché's deception made him *persona non grata* (especially said of a foreign diplomat not acceptable to the host government).

caveat emptor — B: Let the buyer beware; as, When purchasing a used car, remember: *caveat emptor*.

sub rosa — C: Secretly; confidentially; as, to pass on information *sub rosa*.

per diem — D: By the day; daily allowance for expenses; as, The travelling salesman was given a fixed *per diem*.

per se — D: By or in itself; intrinsically; belonging to the basic nature of a person or thing; as, The writer was not a scholar *per se* and made many loose generalisations.

sine qua non — C: Without which there is nothing; indispensable requirement; something essential; as, Love is the *sine qua non* of human existence.

et al. — C: And others; abbreviation of Latin *et alii*; as, my law firm of Harris, Dickson *et al*.

ad nauseam — A: To a sickening or disgusting degree; as, They complained about anything and everything *ad nauseam*.

in extremis — C: At the point of death; in extremity; as, The searchers found the fallen rock climber *in extremis*.

in vitro — D: Artificially maintained in a controlled environment; as, a test-tube baby conceived when an ovum is fertilised *in vitro*. Literally "in glass."

modus operandi — A: Way of working; procedure; as, to discuss a *modus operandi* for company presentations.

ex officio — D: By virtue of office or because of one's position; as, Having expertise in finance, she served *ex officio* on the committee.

quid pro quo — D: Something for something; one thing given in return for another of similar value; as, The negotiator demanded a *quid pro quo*.

status quo — A: Existing condition or situation; as, He was reluctant to disturb the *status quo*.

Vocabulary Ratings
>   9 — 11 correct . . . Good
>   12 — 17 correct . . . Excellent
>   18 — 20 correct . . . Exceptional

66He who does not prevent a crime when he can, encourages it.**99**

—SENECA

IN TOLKIEN'S WORDS

Oxford professor and writer J.R.R. Tolkien, born 105 years ago, won an international cult following with his mythological bestsellers, The Hobbit *and* Lord of the Rings, *from which come the words listed below. Select the word or phrase you believe is nearest in meaning to the key word. Turn the page to find your score.*

allude — A: entice. B: mention. C: avoid. D: forbid.

shrill — A: piercing. B: malicious. C: devout. D: angry.

promontory — A: valley. B: headland. C: walkway. D: private property.

warrant — A: excite. B: conceal. C: guarantee. D: warn.

dire — A: dreadful. B: unruly. C: grimy. D: bold.

incantation — A: public concert. B: prayer. C: firework. D: magic spell.

provender — A: a place of origin. B: fodder. C: descendants. D: sacrifice.

badger — A: put at risk. B: confide. C: pester. D: defy.

famished — A: very hungry. B: jealous. C: hard-hearted. D: exhausted.

allay — A: admit. B: join. C: charm. D: reduce.

sinuous — A: wicked. B: irresistibly powerful. C: genuine. D: curving.

❝We must teach our children to dream with their eyes open.**❞**

—*Harry Edwards, quoted by Dennis Wyss in Time*

WORDS TO THE WISE

Words are small shapes in the gorgeous chaos of the world; shapes that bring the world into focus, corral ideas, hone thoughts. They paint watercolours of perception.

—Diane Ackerman

---

lore — A: traditional knowledge. B: unexpected event. C: essay. D: unfounded rumour.

quake — A: flinch. B: collapse. C: tremble. D: hesitate.

emissary — A: agent. B: refugee. C: hostage. D: important person.

reproachful — A: bloodthirsty. B: disapproving. C: indecisive. D: sociable.

parley — A: discuss terms. B: forgive. C: make a bet. D: ridicule.

perceptible — A: sensitive. B: noticeable. C: unfinished. D: possible.

forsake — A: enforce. B: prepare. C: abandon. D: exclude.

lurk — A: hide. B: stagger. C: spy on. D: cringe.

barrow — A: encampment. B: farmyard. C: lair. D: burial mound.

❝Speak not against anyone whose burden you have not weighed yourself.**❞**

—MARION BRADLEY, BLACK TRILLIUM (DOUBLEDAY)

allude — B: Mention, refer to; as, "*alluding* to him chiefly with a curse." Latin *ad-* (to) and *ludere* (to play).

shrill — A: Piercing, high-pitched. "Gandalf gave a long *shrill* whistle." Germanic *skral-* (sharp).

promontory — B: Headland; as, "a *promontory* of rock which formed a calm bay." Latin *promunturium* (promontory).

warrant — C: Guarantee, state as certainty. "Up to no good, I'll *warrant*!" Old French *warantir* (to guarantee).

dire — A: Dreadful; ominous. "Above him the sleeping dragon lay, a *dire* menace even in his sleep." Latin *dirus* (fearful).

incantation — D: Magic spell. "They could not open it, not though they all pushed while Gandalf tried various *incantations*." Latin *in-* (in) and *cantare* (to sing).

provender — B: Fodder for livestock or, jokingly, for people. "Bringing up young hobbits took a lot of *provender*." Latin *praebenda* (things to be supplied).

badger — C: Pester or torment; as, dogs worrying a badger. "You are always *badgering* me about my ring." Perhaps from Middle English *badge* (distinctive mark).

famished — A: Very hungry. "The hobbits ate, as only *famished* hobbits can eat." Latin *fames* (hunger).

allay — D: Reduce, alleviate; as, "a fear that no words of Saruman could *allay*." Old English *alecgan* (to put down).

sinuous — D: Curving; full of twists and turns. "Out from the water a long *sinuous* tentacle had crawled." Latin *sinus* (fold).

lore — A: Traditional knowledge. "Do not despise the *lore* that has come down from distant years." Old English *lar*.

quake — C: Tremble. "Frodo was hardly less terrified than his companions; he was *quaking* as if he was bitter cold." Old English *cwacian* (to shake).

emissary — **A:** Agent sent on a mission; as, "*emissaries* sent from Mordor to deceive the ignorant." Latin *emissarius* (spy).

reproachful — **B:** Disapproving; censorious. "Various *reproachful* names for himself came to Sam's mind." Latin *re-* (against) and *prope* (near).

parley — **A:** Discuss terms with an enemy. "Will you *parley* with this dealer in treachery and murder?" French *parler* (to speak).

perceptible — **B:** Noticeable, able to be perceived; as, "a tremor of the ground perceptible only to Aragorn as he lay upon the grass." Latin *per-* (through) and *cipere* (to take).

forsake — **C:** Abandon. "We that remain cannot *forsake* our companions while we have strength left." Old English *forsacan* (to deny).

lurk — **A:** Hide, exist unobserved. "Something unpleasant was *lurking* down there, down at the very roots of the mountain." Middle English, perhaps from *loure* (to look dark).

barrow — **D:** Burial mound; as, "the great *barrows* where the sires of Théoden sleep." Old English *beorg* (grave mound).

Vocabulary Ratings

    9 — 11 correct . . . Good
    12 — 17 correct . . . Excellent
    18 — 20 correct . . . Exceptional

66Freedom never yet was given to nations as a gift, but only as a reward, bravely earned by one's own exertions.**99**

—LAJOS KOSSUTH

WORDS TO BANK ON

The following words come from various press commentaries on the banking industry's difficulties. How many of these words can you "bank" on? Mark the answer you think is correct. Turn the page to find your score.

consolidate — A: complete. B: distribute. C: combine. D: offer.

legal tender — A: laundered money. B: bank transaction. C: legitimate currency. D: credit.

arrears — A: privileged knowledge. B: missing inventory. C: extended loan. D: unpaid, overdue debt.

mature — A: past due. B: excessive. C: inactive. D: payable.

promissory note — A: written promise. B: mortgage. C: stock certificate. D: favourable loan.

roll over — A: refinance. B: relax laws. C: negotiate favourably. D: be passive.

point — A: lease. B: bonus to borrower. C: late-payment penalty. D: prepaid interest.

redundant — A: scarce. B: overabundant. C: increasing. D: stagnant.

demand deposit — A: short-term loan. B: mortgage payment. C: cheque or current account. D: reinvestment of interest.

voucher — A: document proving payment. B: statement of financial condition. C: account book. D: withdrawal of money.

❝Never marry for money. Ye'll borrow it cheaper.**❞**

—SCOTTISH PROVERB

> **"** Finance is the art of passing currency from hand to hand until it finally disappears. **"**
>
> —Robert W. Sarnoff, quoted by Malcolm S. Forbes, Sr., in Forbes

---

convertible — A: inconsistent. B: exchangeable. C: shoddy. D: collectible.

liquid assets — valuables that are A: of a floating value. B: volatile. C: suddenly worthless. D: in cash.

debacle — A: complication. B: trickery. C: evil. D: collapse.

par value — A: face amount. B: average cost. C: market equivalent. D: worth at sale.

conveyance — A: compromise. B: legal brief. C: property survey. D: deed.

ire — A: pride. B: pity. C: determination. D: anger.

lien — A: legal claim. B: false statement. C: stock offering. D: sales invoice.

compound interest — interest paid on A: principal. B: bonds. C: principal and unpaid interest. D: stocks.

fungible — A: expendable. B: interchangeable. C: dated. D: mildewed.

sacred cow — anything thought of as A: above criticism. B: unusual. C: well-heeled. D: showy or pompous.

FROM BAD TO VERSE

A bookkeeper, asked to explain
How his fortunes made gain after gain
Said he'd rather not tell
But now he's in a cell—
It was bookkeeping ledger-de-main

—Louis Hasley

ANSWERS

consolidate — C: To combine separate units into a whole. Latin *consolidare* (to make firm).

legal tender — C: Currency that cannot lawfully be refused in payment of an obligation. Latin *legis* (law) and *tendere* (to extend, offer).

arrears — D: Unpaid, overdue debt or obligation; as, Her mortgage payment was two months in *arrears*. Middle English *arrere* (behind).

mature — D: Payable or due; as, a note, loan or bond that becomes *mature*. Latin *maturus* (at full age).

promissory note — A: Written promise to pay a debt at a designated date or on demand. Latin *promissor* (one who promises) and *nota* (mark or sign).

roll over — A: To refinance a maturing obligation by offering a new one of the same type in exchange. Also, to reinvest funds.

point — D: Interest fee, equal to one percent of the loan amount, that is deducted in advance by the lender; as, Many banks no longer charge *points* in granting a mortgage. Latin *punctum* (dot).

redundant — B: Overabundant; more than is needed; as, weeding out *redundant* banks. Latin *redundare* (to overflow).

demand deposit — C: Cheque or current account or similar deposit that may be withdrawn without notice. Latin *demandare* (to entrust) and *deponere* (to put down).

voucher — A: Document proving payment; as, The salesman handed the hotel clerk his room *voucher*. Latin *vocare* (to call).

convertible — B: Exchangeable for something of equal value; as, a *convertible* bond, which on maturity becomes exchangeable for the equivalent in shares of common stock. Latin *convertere* (to turn around).

liquid assets — D: Valuables that are in cash or otherwise quickly convertible into cash. Latin *liquere* (to be fluid) and French *assez* (enough).

debacle — D: Disastrous collapse; humiliating failure; as, Many families lost their life savings in the Wall Street *debacle* of 1929. French *debacler* (to break up).

par value — A: Face amount of a security at the time of issue; as, The bank's holdings were under *par value*. Latin *par* (equal) and *valere* (to be worth).

conveyance — D: Deed; transference of property ownership, especially as real estate. Latin *conviare*.

ire — D: Anger; as, Unscrupulous businessmen raised his *ire*. Latin *ira*.

lien — A: Legal claim to take, hold or sell property of a person who owes money; as, a *lien* on a builder's assets. Latin *ligare* (to bind).

compound interest — C: Interest paid on both principal and the accumulated unpaid interest. Latin *componere* (to put together) and *interesse*.

fungible — B: Interchangeable and equivalent in value to satisfy an obligation; as, Gold bullion and the equivalent dollars are *fungible*. Latin *fungi* (to perform).

sacred cow — A: Anything thought of as above, or immune to, criticism; as, Many people thought of banks as *sacred cows*. From the Hindu practice of venerating cows.

Vocabulary Ratings
> 9 — 11 correct . . . Good
> 12 — 17 correct . . . Excellent
> 18 — 20 correct . . . Exceptional

66Money is flat and meant to be piled up.**99**
—SCOTTISH PROVERB

EN ROUTE

Just as a propeller drives a ship ahead, the "fy" ending on a word impels it forward. "Fy" comes from the Latin facere *(to make). Turn the page to find out if these twenty verbs have helped you move forward on your route to a larger, more effective vocabulary.*

certify — A: verify. B: claim. C: issue a licence. D: list.

vilify — A: shame. B: slander. C: confront. D: lie.

personify — A: popularise. B: be friendly. C: state boldly.
D: typify.

amplify — A: satisfy. B: round off. C: increase. D: prolong.

indemnify — A: accuse. B: bring to trial. C: protect.
D: challenge or oppose.

stultify — A: be stubborn. B: make ineffective. C: harden.
D: shrink to unusable size.

quantify — A: measure. B: empower. C: excuse oneself.
D: add to.

stupefy — A: strengthen. B: frustrate. C: cripple. D: dull.

codify — A: translate. B: make firm. C: systematise. D: explain.

deify — A: commemorate. B: idealise. C: preserve.
D: exaggerate.

exemplify — A: discuss. B: imitate. C: illustrate. D: punish.

❝Determine that the thing can and shall be done, and
then we shall find the way.**❞**

—ABRAHAM LINCOLN

> **66** He that would be a leader must be a bridge. **99**
>
> —WELSH PROVERB

---

sanctify — A: consecrate. B: become quiet. C: be in seclusion. D: grow in religious fervour.

transmogrify — A: transform. B: be in a hypnotic sleep. C: disintegrate. D: be in distress.

nullify — A: retreat. B: even out. C: question. D: cancel.

reify — A: make louder. B: reinforce continually. C: treat an abstract as a tangible. D: become more elegant.

justify — A: put into law. B: substantiate. C: quibble about. D: gloss over.

mortify — A: humiliate. B: exasperate. C: exterminate. D: give in to.

minify — A: lessen. B: extend. C: calm. D: work carefully.

gentrify — A: impoverish. B: farm as a hobby. C: upgrade. D: be excessively polite.

edify — A: admire. B: uplift. C: enjoy. D: be diligent.

ROAD SHOWS

On outskirts of small town: "Welcome, speeders! We're policed to meet you!"

—LEONARD BOSSARD

"Cross road ahead—better humour it."

—BENNETT CERF

On a marquee: "Don't learn traffic laws by accident."

—HILDEGARDE REVAK

certify — A: Verify; confirm as true and accurate; guarantee; as, to have a cashier *certify* that the signature is yours. Latin *certus* (certain).

vilify — B: Slander; make vicious statements about; blacken a good name; as, The surprise witness lied and *vilified* the two defendants. Latin *vilis* (cheap, base).

personify — D: Typify; represent; embody; as, To her students, Miss Rodgers *personified* the ideal teacher. Old French *persone* (person).

amplify — C: Increase or make stronger; as, The floods *amplified* the earthquake's devastation. Also, to add details or illustrations for clarity. Latin *amplus* (large).

indemnify — C: Protect against future damage; insure; as, to *indemnify* oneself against a car accident. Also, to compensate for loss. Latin *indemnis* (uninjured).

stultify — B: Make ineffective; impair; reduce to futility; as, Over-reliance on rote drill can *stultify* a student's ability to learn. Latin *stultus* (foolish).

quantify — A: Measure; determine or indicate the extent of; as, to try to *quantify* the amount of pollution in the air. Latin *quantus* (how much).

stupefy — D: Dull, stun or daze from shock, fatigue or narcotics; as, News of the disaster *stupefied* the victims' relatives. Also, to amaze. Latin *stupere* (to be stunned).

codify — C: Systematise laws, rules or regulations into a collection or code; as, to *codify* a town's building regulations. Latin *codex* (tablet on which laws were written).

deify — B: Idealise; exalt; glorify; make a god of; as, rock stars *deified* by their fans. Latin *deus* (god).

exemplify — C: Illustrate; show or serve as an example; as, *Tom Sawyer* is a novel that *exemplifies* small-town nineteenth-century American life. Medieval Latin *exemplum* (example).

sanctify — A: Consecrate; set apart as holy; as, to *sanctify* a burial ground. Also, to give religious sanction to, as in marriage vows. Latin *sanctus* (holy).

transmogrify — A: Transform; change completely in a fantastic or grotesque way; as, Dr. Jekyll was *transmogrified* into the monstrous Mr. Hyde. Origin unknown.

nullify — D: Cancel; annul; make legally void; as, to *nullify* an agreement. Also, to make useless; as, New technologies often *nullify* older styles of management. Latin *nullus* (none).

reify — C: Treat an abstraction as if it had a concrete or tangible existence; as, Some physicists *reify* the concept of space-time. Latin *res* (thing).

justify — B: Substantiate; vindicate; as, to *justify* a budget. Also, to defend or absolve; as, Don't *justify* her rudeness. Latin *justus* (just, fair).

mortify — A: Humiliate greatly; cause shame or wounded pride; as, The spelling-bee winner was *mortified* by confusing "principle" with "principal." Latin *mors* (death).

minify — A: Lessen; reduce in size or importance; as, Never *minify* their contribution. Latin *min* (less).

gentrify — C: Upgrade a neighbourhood by renovating homes; as, to *gentrify* the east end of the city. English *gentry*.

edify — B: Uplift; encourage intellectual, moral and spiritual growth; as, Good books can *edify* the mind. Latin *aedes* (dwelling).

Vocabulary Ratings

9 — 11 correct . . . Good

12 — 17 correct . . . Excellent

18 — 20 correct . . . Exceptional

EUREKA!

Bright ideas depend above all on a strong vocabulary to give them lasting brilliance. How many of the following words light up your face with understanding? Turn the page for your results.

resolve — A: self-reliance. B: wilfulness. C: determination. D: protest.

comprehend — A: examine. B: puzzle over. C: grasp mentally. D: consider.

premise — A: summary. B: pledge. C: proven fact. D: assumption.

demonstrable — A: overwhelming. B: emotional. C: showy. D: evident.

reflective — A: thoughtful. B: slow. C: responsive. D: watchful.

plausible — A: easily changed. B: seemingly true. C: authoritative. D: effective.

scrutiny — A: angry glance. B: cleanliness. C: caution. D: close examination.

envision — A: explain. B: remember. C: imagine. D: encompass.

affirmation — A: firmness. B: dissension. C: approbation. D: confirmation.

practicable — A: feasible. B: businesslike. C: experimental. D: influential.

curriculum — A: scheme or method. B: courses of study. C: end point. D: resource.

❝Education is not the filling of a pail, but the lighting of a fire.❞

—WILLIAM BUTLER YEATS

> **"**Knowledge is power, but enthusiasm
> pulls the switch.**"**
>
> —IVERN BALL IN NATIONAL ENQUIRER

infrastructure — A: foundation. B: political
    action committee. C: separation
    of powers. D: insiders' group.
initiate — A: check off. B: review. C: begin.
    D: be enthusiastic.
inference — A: concept. B: accusation. C: representation.
    D: reasoned conclusion.
optimal — A: promising. B: best. C: not compulsory.
    D: harmless.
sagacious — A: wise. B: heroic. C: fair-minded. D: elderly.
compensatory — A: counterbalancing. B: regulated.
    C: punishing. D: unjust.
impasse — A: impractical condition. B: confrontation.
    C: bewilderment. D: stalemate.
probity — A: procedure. B: honesty. C: legislative inquiry.
    D: self-righteousness.
lucid — A: easily understood. B: colourful. C: without sense.
    D: highly intelligent.

> **"**A person often meets his destiny on the road
> he took to avoid it.**"**
>
> —JEAN DE LA FONTAINE

 ANSWERS

resolve — C: Determination; firmness of purpose; as, She kept to her *resolve*. Latin *resolvere* (to unfasten, loosen).

comprehend — C: Grasp mentally; understand; as, He failed to *comprehend* the importance of the concept. Latin *comprehendere* (to grasp).

premise — D: Assumption; proposition or belief taken for granted but not proved; as, a strategy based on a faulty *premise*. Latin *praemittere* (to send before).

demonstrable — D: Clearly evident; able to be shown or authenticated; as, a *demonstrable* need to improve the quality of education. Latin *demonstrare* (to indicate).

reflective — A: Thoughtful; analytical; pensive; as, *Reflective* parents often avoid hasty reactions to their unruly children. Latin *reflectere* (to bend back).

plausible — B: Seemingly true or reasonable, though more proof is desirable; as, He gave *plausible* reasons for the change in plans. Latin *plaudere* (to applaud).

scrutiny — D: Close examination or searching study; as, The proposal is under the committee's *scrutiny*. Latin *scrutari* (to search).

envision — C: Imagine or picture in the mind, especially a future event; as, to *envision* a world at peace. English *en-* (cause) and *vision*.

affirmation — D: Confirmation or assertion that something is true; as, an *affirmation* of serious plans to reduce the deficit. Latin *affirmare* (to present as firm).

practicable — A: Feasible; capable of being done or put into practice; as, a *practicable* economic policy. Greek *praktikos* (practical).

curriculum — B: Courses of study offered in schools; as, to change a school's *curriculum*. Latin (a running contest).

infrastructure — A: Foundation; basic facilities needed for the functioning of a system, as a community's roads, schools or transportation system. Latin *infra* (below) and *structure*.

initiate — C: Begin; originate; as, his designs *initiate* fashion trends. Also, to teach the fundamentals of a subject. Latin *initiare*.

inference — D: Conclusion arrived at by reasoning based on known facts. Latin *inferre* (to bring in).

optimal — B: Best or most favourable; as, an *optimal* timing for the summit meeting. Latin *optimus*.

sagacious — A: Wise; having a keenly perceptive mind, good judgement and sound, practical sense; as, a *sagacious* judge. Latin *sagire* (to perceive quickly).

compensatory — A: Counterbalancing; making up for a loss; as, *compensatory* payment for damages. Latin *compensare*.

impasse — D: Stalemate; any deadlock; as, International trade negotiations failed to break the *impasse*. French.

probity — B: Uncompromising honesty; proven integrity; as, a beloved queen known for her *probity*. Latin *probus*.

lucid — A: Easily understood; clearly expressed; as, *lucid* instructions. Latin *lucere* (to shine, glitter).

Vocabulary Ratings
9 — 11 correct ... Good
12 — 17 correct ... Excellent
18 — 20 correct ... Exceptional

❝The difference between the impossible and the possible lies in a person's determination.**❞**

—TOMMY LASORDA

NAMES THAT LAST

Want to make yourself immortal? Get your name published in the dictionary—as did Louis Braille and Captain Charles C. Boycott, among others. Their names have become eponyms—names synonymous with an invention, action or product. How many of these do you recognise? Turn the page for the answers and your score.

dunce — person who is A: disobedient. B: spry. C: dull-witted.
D: innocent.

ampere — unit for measuring A: electricity. B: water flow. C: light.
D: heat.

leotard — A: headband. B: ballet slipper. C: close-fitting garment.
D: long silk scarf.

mausoleum — A: Turkish rug. B: large urn. C: town square.
D: tomb.

Parthian shot — A: nonalcoholic drink. B: style of dress.
C: hostile remark. D: dilapidated auto.

maudlin — A: forgetful. B: sensitive. C: gentle and kind.
D: foolishly sentimental.

mesmerise — A: polish. B: bewilder. C: daydream.
D: hypnotise.

Lucullan — A: narrow-minded. B: widespread. C: light-filled.
D: sumptuous.

chauvinistic — A: warm and friendly. B: manly. C: smug,
superior in attitude. D: extremely stubborn.

shrapnel — A: perfume. B: shrub. C: scattered fragments.
D: booster rocket.

❝The glory of great men should always be measured by the
means they have used to acquire it.**❞**

—LA ROCHEFOUCAULD

CELEBRITY QUIZ

Will Donald Trump my ace? —Dorothy Damon
How many deals did Glenn Close? —Jean Wiggin
How did Tina Turner career around? —Chris Fisher and Ben MacKay

platonic — A: ambitious. B: without envy. C: constant.
D: spiritual or intellectual.

draconian — A: horse-like. B: frightening. C: harsh. D: dreary.

Doppler effect — change in A: potency of a sedative.
B: sound frequencies. C: wheel traction. D: sleep patterns.

Caesarean — A: surgical procedure. B: political skill.
C: leadership. D: winning attitude.

martinet — A: bird lover. B: hero. C: puppet.
D: strict disciplinarian.

Pyrrhic victory — one that is A: overwhelming.
B: gained at great cost. C: quick. D: won by a few over many.

Machiavellian — A: crafty. B: weird. C: straightforward.
D: practical.

maverick — A: wanderer. B: sly cheat. C: nonconformist.
D: loyal servant.

spoonerism — A: secret romance. B: slip of the tongue.
C: hobby of collecting antiques. D: baby talk.

cardigan — A: emblem. B: knitted jacket. C: type of wool.
D: skirt.

66 No steam or gas drives anything until it is confined. No life ever grows great until it is focused, dedicated, disciplined. 99

—HARRY EMERSON FOSDICK, LIVING UNDER TENSION (HARPERCOLLINS)

dunce — C: Dull-witted or ignorant person. Used by Renaissance humanists to ridicule followers of John *Duns* Scotus (1265?–1308), a Scottish theologian.

ampere — A: Standard unit for measuring the strength of electric current; as, a fifteen-*ampere* fuse. Named after French physicist André Marie *Ampère* (1775–1836).

leotard — C: Close-fitting, one-piece garment. After Jules *Léotard*, a nineteenth-century French aerialist.

mausoleum — D: Magnificent tomb; large, gloomy building. After the tomb for King *Mausolus*, fourth-century B.C., one of the seven wonders of the ancient world.

Parthian shot — C: Hostile remark or gesture delivered while departing. From the custom of third-century B.C. Parthian archers who shot their arrows backwards while retreating.

maudlin — D: Foolishly sentimental; emotional. Old French *Madeleine* for *Mary Magdalene*, a follower of Christ often portrayed as weeping.

mesmerise — D: To hypnotise, spellbind, enchant. After German physician Franz Anton *Mesmer* (1734–1815).

Lucullan — D: Sumptuous or lavish, usually pertaining to banquets; as, *Lucullan* meals on cruise ships. After Lucius Lucinius *Lucullus* (110?–57? B.C.), a Roman general famous for staging elaborate banquets.

chauvinistic — C: Smug, superior in attitude as to race, sex or nationality; as, *chauvinistic* women or men. Also, fanatically patriotic. From Nicolas *Chauvin*, a French soldier fiercely loyal to Napoleon.

shrapnel — C: Scattered fragments from an exploding shell or bomb. After Henry *Shrapnel* (1761–1842), a British artillery officer.

platonic — D: Spiritual or intellectual; non-sexual; especially as describes a close relationship between a man and a woman. After *Plato*, Greek philosopher (fourth-century B.C.).

draconian — C: Very harsh; unusually severe or cruel; as, *draconian* punishment for dissenters. After *Draco*, Greek lawmaker (seventh-century B.C.).

Doppler effect — B: Change in the pitch of sound, to higher frequencies when the source approaches and lower as it recedes, as with a train whistle. After Austrian physicist Christian *Doppler* (1803–53).

Caesarean — A: Surgical operation to deliver a baby—called a *Caesarean* section in medical terminology. From the folklore surrounding Julius *Caesar*'s birth.

martinet — D: Strict disciplinarian; as, Our Army sergeant was a *martinet*. After the seventeenth-century French drillmaster Jean *Martinet*.

Pyrrhic victory — B: Victory achieved at such great cost that it is nearly a defeat. From the victory of *Pyrrhus*, king of Epirus, over the Romans (279 B.C.).

Machiavellian — A: Crafty, deceitful or amoral; as, *Machiavellian* political intrigue. After the Florentine writer Nicolò *Machiavelli* (1469–1527).

maverick — C: Nonconformist; person with unorthodox or independent views. After Samuel *Maverick* (1803–70), a Texas rancher who chose not to brand his cattle.

spoonerism — B: Slip of the tongue; as, calling a "well-oiled bicycle" a "well-boiled icicle." After the Rev. William A. *Spooner* (1844–1930), who was noted for such slips.

cardigan — B: Knitted jacket or sweater with buttons up the front. After the seventh Earl of *Cardigan* (1797–1868), a British general.

Vocabulary Ratings

>   9 — 11 correct ... Good
>   12 — 17 correct ... Excellent
>   18 — 20 correct ... Exceptional

WORLDS OF OPPORTUNITIES

Newly learned words can carry you, like a glider caught in an updraft, to greater heights of understanding. The following terms are drawn from news of economic opportunities opened up by recent world changes. Select the answers you think are correct, then turn the page for your score.

ethic — A: standard of behaviour. B: racial group. C: precision. D: reliability.

plague — A: surround. B: harass. C: implore. D: look on the dark side.

battery — A: forceful protest. B: hodgepodge accumulation. C: group of similar objects. D: encirclement.

renege — A: snub. B: play the maverick. C: take control. D: back out.

fait accompli — A: sophisticated approach. B: well-planned action. C: finishing touch. D: accomplished fact.

stagflation — A: controlled prices. B: economic slowdown. C: a disintegrating government. D: cultural dullness.

scuttle — A: tease. B: abandon. C: pile up. D: gossip.

procure — A: obtain. B: soothe. C: remedy. D: transport.

anomaly — A: unnamed quality. B: likeness. C: response. D: abnormality.

“Industry is a better horse to ride than genius.”

—WALTER LIPPMANN, USED WITH PERMISSION OF HARVARD UNIVERSITY

> **"** Those who expect to reap the blessings of freedom must undergo the fatigue of supporting it. **"**
>
> —THOMAS PAINE

---

contravention — A: anarchy. B: deception. C: political gathering.
  D: violation.

feckless — A: faithless. B: relaxed. C: ineffective.
  D: without a fault.

pan- — a prefix meaning A: part. B: around. C: all. D: against.

rapport — A: detailed account. B: sympathetic relationship.
  C: period of tension. D: completion.

brassy — A: bold. B: hardheaded. C: sensitive.
  D: highly visible.

murky — A: unclear. B: harsh. C: conspiring. D: borderline.

stanch — A: reinforce. B: be weak. C: smooth out.
  D: put an end to.

guise — A: outward appearance. B: superficiality.
  C: normal procedure. D: slyness.

skittish — A: amusing. B: jumpy. C: sliding. D: inconclusive.

sui generis — A: unique. B: suitable. C: outdated.
  D: of one people.

belated — A: complaining. B: offhand. C: weak. D: tardy.

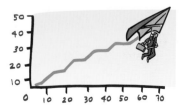

ethic — A: Standard of behaviour; set of moral, personal or cultural values; as, the Japanese work *ethic*. Greek *ethikos* (character).

plague — B: Harass, trouble, vex, torment mentally; as, The company has been *plagued* by a shortage of money. Latin *plaga* (wound; affliction).

battery — C: Group of similar objects used together for a common purpose; as, a *battery* of restrictions. French *battre* (to beat).

renege — D: Back out; not keep one's promise or word; as, If one country *reneges* on an agreement, should the other? Latin *re-* (again) and *negare* (to deny).

fait accompli — D: Accomplished fact; thing already done; as, The plan for joint production of the FSX plane is a *fait accompli*. French.

stagflation — B: An economic slowdown when inflation occurs, unemployment rises and business activity declines. Economic jargon combining stagnation and inflation.

scuttle — B: Abandon; withdraw from an undertaking; as, to *scuttle* hopes for a multinational pact. Spanish *escotilla* (hatchway).

procure — A: Obtain or bring about by effort or a scheme; as, Equipment was *procured* from local manufacturers. Latin *procurare* (to take care of).

anomaly — D: Abnormality; deviation from the expected; irregularity; as, Cuba's hard-line communism is now an *anomaly*. Greek *anomalia* (inequality).

contravention — D: Violation; opposition; as, The agreement was a *contravention* of free-trade principles. Latin *contra-* (against) and *venire* (to come).

feckless — C: Ineffective; irresponsible; incompetent; as, *feckless* economic policies of the socialists. Scottish *feck* (effect) and English *-less* (without).

pan- — C: A combining prefix meaning all, every, universal; as, A *pan*-European operation. Greek.

rapport — B: Sympathetic relationship; as, growing *rapport* between former enemies. French (harmony, agreement).

brassy — A: Shamelessly bold; insolent; impudent; as, innovative ideas from that *brassy* economist. From English *brass*.

murky — A: Unclear; confused; vague; as, The marketing strategy seems *murky*. Also, dark; gloomy. Middle English *mirky*.

stanch — D: Put an end to; stop a flow of blood or resources; as, America's low savings rate must rise to *stanch* reliance on credit. Middle English *stanchen*.

guise — A: Outward appearance, aspect or manner; as, seeing Hungary in a new *guise*. Also, pretence. French.

skittish — B: Jumpy, easily frightened; unpredictable; as, the *skittish* bond market. Dialectal English.

sui generis — A: Unique; unparalleled; having no equal; as, Due to revolutionary political changes, the economic situation in Eastern Europe is *sui generis*. Latin (of its own kind).

belated — D: Tardy; delayed; coming too late; as, In a *belated* decision, the Germans adopted the policy. English *be-* (completely) and *late*.

Vocabulary Ratings
> 9 — 11 correct . . . Good
> 12 — 17 correct . . . Excellent
> 18 — 20 correct . . . Exceptional

"Be wary of the man who urges an action in which he himself incurs no risk.**"**

—*Joaquin Setanti*

IMPORTS AND EXPORTS

International trade involves words as well as goods and services. How many of the "import" words that follow do you know? Turn the page for your score.

tariff — A: tax. B: payoff. C: warning. D: price increase.

sarong — A: headband. B: bathing suit. C: loose skirt. D: shawl.

kismet — A: patience. B: fate. C: resentment. D: love.

nadir — A: faint shadow. B: subtlety. C: lowest point. D: evil spirit.

armada — A: row of statues. B: cabinet. C: fleet of ships. D: crowd.

Adonis — A: handsome youth. B: swift runner. C: hero. D: hunter.

sierra — A: midday rest. B: place of wealth and opportunity. C: desert. D: mountain range.

facile — A: careful. B: versatile. C: superficial. D: convincing.

kibitz — A: settle in. B: offer advice. C: insult. D: chitchat.

Wunderkind — A: kindly person. B: acrobat. C: film star. D: child prodigy.

❝What a wonderful thing is the mail, capable of conveying across continents a warm human handclasp.**❞**

—*Quoted by Ranjan Bakshi*

NATIVE TONGUES

An Irish brogue thick enough to plant shamrocks in.

—Bernie Ward in Sky

A German accent with enough old-world elegance to make even a casual conversation seem bound in fine leather.

—Carlin Romano in *The Washington Post*

---

peccadillo — A: slight fault. B: irritability. C: musical instrument. D: bullfighter's lance.

lampoon — A: decorative furniture. B: word puzzle. C: unexplained event. D: satire.

chutzpah — A: concern. B: aloofness. C: shameless audacity. D: inside joke.

debut — A: conclusion. B: contradiction. C: gracious response. D: first appearance.

Gesundheit — A: "your health." B: "surprise!" C: "bless you." D. "heavens!"

vendetta — A: dishonesty. B: mall. C: feud. D: meeting.

leitmotif — A: sadness. B: fantasy. C: recurring theme. D: lighthearted romance.

origami — art form involving A: wood. B: fabric. C: paper. D: gardening.

taboo — A: mystery. B: ancient tale. C: prohibition. D: prank.

smithereens — A: list. B: broken pieces. C: hodgepodge. D: garments.

66Liberty, when it begins to take root, is a plant of rapid growth.**99**

—GEORGE WASHINGTON

 *ANSWERS*

tariff — A: Export or import tax or duty levied by a government; as, a conference on trade and *tariffs*. Arabic *ta'rif* (information).

sarong — C: Loose skirt of coloured cloth worn by Malaysian men and women. Malay (sheath).

kismet — B: Fate; destiny; as, She looked lovingly into his eyes and said, "Our meeting here must be *kismet*." Arabic *qismah* (portion, lot).

nadir — C: Lowest point; time of deepest depression; as, the *nadir* of despair. Arabic *nazir as-samt* (opposite to the zenith).

armada — C: Fleet of warships or aircraft; as, the international *armada* in the Persian Gulf. Spanish.

Adonis — A: Handsome youth. In Greek mythology a young man loved by Aphrodite, goddess of love and beauty.

sierra — D: Mountain range, especially one having a jagged, saw-like appearance; as, They went hiking in the *Sierra* Nevada. Spanish (saw).

facile — C: Superficial; without depth; as, His too *facile* excuse seemed phony. Also, effortless, dexterous; as, the *facile* fingers of a violinist. French.

kibitz — B: Volunteer advice that is neither sought nor wanted; as, He watched them play cards, annoying everyone with his *kibitzing*. Yiddish.

Wunderkind — D: Child prodigy; young, outstandingly successful person; as, The scientist, a *Wunderkind*, explored the theory of chaos. German (wonder child).

peccadillo — A: Slight or trifling fault; as, her *peccadillo* of talking too long on the telephone. Spanish.

lampoon — D: Satire; whatever humorously exposes foolishness; as, As a controversial public figure, he was the frequent subject of *lampoons*. French, from the refrain of a seventeenth-century drinking song—*lampons* (let us drink).

chutzpah — C: Shameless audacity; impudence; as, He exhibited amazing *chutzpah*; accused of swindling, he not only denied it but blamed someone else. Yiddish.

debut — D: First public appearance; beginning; as, her *debut* as a concert pianist. French *débuter* (to lead off).

Gesundheit — A: "Your health," used as an expression of good wishes to someone who has just sneezed. German.

vendetta — C: Prolonged, bitter feud with continuing acts of vengeance. Italian (revenge).

leitmotif — C: Recurring theme in music or writing associated with a character or emotion; as, Richard Wagner made extensive use of *leitmotifs* in his music. German.

origami — C: Traditional Japanese art of folding paper to fashion flowers, people, animals and other forms. From *ori* (fold) and *kami* (paper).

taboo — C: Prohibition; sacred ban excluding something from mention or use; as, Certain words or actions in some settings are *taboo*. From the Polynesian language Tongan.

smithereens — B: Small, broken pieces or fragments; as, The vase fell to the floor, breaking into *smithereens*. Irish Gaelic *smidirin*.

Vocabulary Ratings
>   9 — 11 correct . . . Good
>   12 — 17 correct . . . Excellent
>   18 — 20 correct . . . Exceptional

❝When goods do not cross borders, soldiers will.**❞**

—FRÉDÉRIC BASTIAT

ACCENTS OF INDIA

*All of these borrowings from India—the land of Himalayas,
maharajas and Bengal tigers—enliven the English language and
weave colourful threads through our familiar talk and writing.
How many of these nouns do you know? Turn the page to find out.*

atoll — A: arched passageway. B: island of volcanic rock.
    C: ring-shaped coral island. D: life buoy.

veranda — A: rooftop widow's walk. B: inner courtyard.
    C: broad view. D: large, mostly open porch.

mogul — A: traitor. B: powerful or influential person. C: trap.
    D: man of gigantic stature.

sari — A: gentle breeze. B: place of refuge. C: hand-pulled cart.
    D: woman's garment.

mufti — A: civilian clothes. B: coarse fibre. C: military uniform.
    D: hand-warmer.

calico — A: bright colour. B: fine silk. C: stuffed toy.
    D: cotton cloth.

pagoda — A: garden walkway. B: small wooden bridge. C: temple.
    D: country palace.

pundit — person who is A: argumentative. B: boring. C: witty.
    D: learned.

jodhpurs — A: running clothes. B: work overalls. C: riding
    breeches. D: turret-like structures.

EXPRESS WAYS

A weaver of tales, he shuttled words back and forth across

the loom of his imagination.

—PATRICIA O. GRADY

maharishi — A: dried flower petals. B: prince. C: fish delicacy. D: religious teacher.

cummerbund — A: binding agreement. B: clumsy mistake. C: sash worn at the waist. D: solemn ceremony.

dinghy — A: eccentric person. B: washbasin. C: set of bells. D: small boat.

Brahmin — A: judge. B: elderly wise person. C: aristocrat. D: statesman.

chukker — A: game played with tiles. B: time period in polo. C: fruit relish. D: exercise ball.

nabob — A: wealthy person. B: social worker. C: game played with coins. D: elephant trainer.

nirvana — A: state of peace. B: extreme exhaustion. C: fate. D: hopelessness.

mantra — A: cloak. B: ornament. C: deep-sea fish. D: incantation.

bangle — A: drum. B: temple bell. C: bracelet. D: wind chime.

chit — A: gossip. B: voucher. C: trick. D: tool.

pariah — A: outcast. B: Hindu ruler. C: head of a family. D: canopy.

❝Every child comes with the message that God is not yet discouraged of man.**❞**

—RABINDRANATH TAGORE

atoll — C: Ring-shaped coral island and reef enclosing a lagoon. From *atolu*, native word for the Maldive Islands.

veranda — D: Large, roofed and usually open porch, often extending across the front and sides of a house. Hindi *varanda*.

mogul — B: Powerful or influential person. After the 16th- to 18th-century Mongolian conquerors of India.

sari — D: Garment, worn by Hindu women, draped so that one end forms a skirt and the other covers the shoulders or head. Hindi.

mufti — A: Informal clothing worn by off-duty officials; hence, civilian garb. Cloth gown worn by a *mufti* (religious judge) in Moslem countries. From Arabic.

calico — D: A cotton cloth. From Calicut, India, where it was first exported.

pagoda — C: Pyramid-like temple with an odd number of stories, often built over a sacred relic. Sanskrit *bhagavati* (goddess, divinity).

pundit — D: Learned person; one who is supposedly an authority on a subject. Hindi *pandit*.

jodhpurs — C: Riding breeches, closely fitted from knee to ankle. From *Jodhpur*, India, where they first became popular.

maharishi — D: Hindu religious teacher. Sanskrit *maharsi* (great sage).

cummerbund — C: Wide sash worn as a waistband by men in India and adapted in Western countries for formal wear with tuxedos or dinner jackets. Hindi *kamarband*.

dinghy — D: Any small boat used as a lifeboat or yacht tender. In India, a rowing-boat. Hindi *dingi*.

Brahmin — C: Aristocrat; highly cultured or intellectually aloof person. In India, a high-caste Hindu.

chukker — B: One of the time periods in polo, a game played by teams on horseback. Hindi *chakkar* from Sanskrit *cakra* (wheel).

nabob — A: Very wealthy, important person. Hindi *nawab* (official under the Mogul empire—from 1526 to 1757—in India).

nirvana — A: State of transcendental peace. For Hindus and Buddhists, freedom from suffering, desire and earthly attachments, when the soul is absorbed into the Supreme Being. Sanskrit (a blowing out).

mantra — D: Incantation; a sacred phrase chanted or intoned to help one's spiritual concentration. Sanskrit (sacred counsel).

bangle — C: Bracelet worn around the wrist or ankle. Hindi *bangri* (glass bracelet).

chit — B: Voucher for a small sum of money owed to the bearer, as for food. Hindi *chitthi* (letter, note).

pariah — A: Social outcast; despised person. Tamil *paraiyan* (drummer). In India, those who played the drums were members of a low caste.

Vocabulary Ratings

9 — 11 correct . . . Good
12 — 17 correct . . . Excellent
18 — 20 correct . . . Exceptional

SANSKRIT PROVERB

Look to this day
For yesterday is but a dream,
And tomorrow is only a vision,
But today, well lived,
Makes every yesterday a dream of happiness
And every tomorrow a vision of hope.
Look well, therefore, to this day.

IMPROVING WITH AGE

"A soft answer turns away wrath," says the book of *Proverbs*. And this book of the Bible contains many words of wisdom every bit as pertinent today as when they were first set down nearly three thousand years ago. So, *"get wisdom; get insight"* (4:5). And turn the page to check your score.

diligent — A: honest. B: hard-working. C: humourless. D: watchful.

prudence — A: cautious judgement. B: fussiness. C: morality. D: traditional practice.

devious — A: thoughtless. B: laid-back. C: complicated. D: deceitful.

garland — A: spice. B: wreath. C: ringlet. D: flower garden.

cistern — A: stream. B: culvert. C: tank. D: tube.

sluggard — person who is A: foolish. B: pugnacious. C: awkward. D: lazy.

vexation — A: annoyance. B: slyness. C: unfriendliness. D: fright.

lattice — A: enclosure. B: covering. C: head decoration. D: shutter.

vapour — A: breeze. B: ointment. C: mist. D: whimsy.

countenance — A: reliability. B: facial expression. C: antagonism. D: behaviour.

❝You can send a message around the world in one-fifth of a second, yet it may take years for it to get from the outside of a man's head to the inside.**❞**

—CHARLES F. KETTERING

---

repute — A: reputation. B: gossip. C: denial. D: illicit business.

provocation — A: solemn statement. B: something that incites.
C: gloomy prediction. D: inclination.

abhor — A: detest. B: refuse to acknowledge.
C: treat shamefully. D: put an end to.

meddle — A: force. B: interfere. C: confuse. D: mix.

importune — A: insult. B: convince. C: criticise. D: beg.

crucible — A: cross. B: piece of jewellery. C: heat-resistant
container. D: buttress.

reproof — A: addition confirmation. B: expression of disapproval.
C: silence. D: violent agitation.

envoy — A: messenger. B: escort. C: royal attendant.
D: introduction.

surety — A: equilibrium. B: faithfulness. C: determination.
D: guarantee.

exalt — A: sing. B: boast. C: glorify. D: leap.

 ANSWERS

diligent — B: Hard-working; painstakingly careful; as, ". . . the soul of the *diligent* is richly supplied" (Proverbs 13:4). Latin *diligere* (to esteem, choose).

prudence — A: Cautious good judgement; as, ". . . that *prudence* may be given to the simple, knowledge and discretion to the youth" (1:4). Latin *prudentia* (foresight).

devious — D: Deceitful; shifty; as, "He who walks in unrightness fears the Lord, but he who is *devious* in his ways despises him" (14:2). Latin *devius* (off the road).

garland — B: Wreath of flowers used as decoration or as a symbol of honour; as, "[Your father's instruction and mother's teaching] a fair *garland* for your head" (1:9). Old French *garlande*.

cistern — C: Tank for collecting rainwater; as, "Drink water from your own *cistern*" (5:15). Latin *cisterna* (underground reservoir).

sluggard — D: Lazy person; loafer; idler; as, "Go to the ant, O *sluggard*; consider her ways, and be wise" (6:6). Middle English *slogarde*.

vexation — A: Annoyance; irritation; as, "The *vexation* of a fool is known at once, but the prudent man ignores an insult" (12:16). Latin *vexatio*.

lattice — D: Shutter, trellis of crossed strips; as, "For at the window of my house I have looked out through my *lattice*" (7:6). Old French *lattis*.

vapour — C: Mist or fog; as, "The getting of treasures by a lying tongue is a fleeting *vapour* and a snare of death" (21:6). Latin.

countenance — B: Facial expression showing one's feelings; as, "A glad heart makes a cheerful *countenance*" (15:13). Old French *contenance* (conduct).

repute — A: Reputation; as, ". . . do not disclose another's secret; lest he who hears you bring shame upon you, and your ill *repute* have no end" (25:10). Latin *reputare* (to think over).

provocation — B: Something that incites or angers; as, "A stone is heavy, and sand is weighty, but a fool's *provocation* is heavier than both" (27:3). Latin *provocare* (to call forth).

abhor — A: Detest; regard with disgust or horror; as, "He who says to the wicked, 'You are innocent,' will be . . . *abhorred* by nations" (24:24). Latin *abhorrere* (to shrink from).

meddle — B: Interfere needlessly in others' affairs; as, "He who *meddles* in a quarrel not his own is like one who takes a passing dog by the ears" (26:17). Old French *medler* (to mix).

importune — D: Beg with persistent urgency; as, ". . . you have come into your neighbour's power: go, hasten, and *importune* your neighbour" (6:3). Latin *importunus* (unsuitable).

crucible — C: Heat-resistant container in which materials are melted; also, a severe test; as, "The *crucible* is for silver . . . and a man is judged by his praise" (27:21). Medieval Latin *crucibulum* (night lamp).

reproof — B: Expression of disapproval; rebuke; as, "Give heed to my *reproof*" (1:23). Old French *reprouver*.

envoy — A: Messenger; government representative of a diplomatic mission; as, ". . . a faithful *envoy* brings healing" (13:17). Old French (a sending).

surety — D: Guarantee; person responsible for another; as, "Be not one of those who give pledges, who become *surety* for debts" (22:26). Latin *securus* (sure; free from fears).

exalt — C: Glorify; praise; lift up; as, "Righteousness *exalts* a nation" (14:34). Latin *exaltare* (to lift up).

Vocabulary Ratings

> 9 — 11 correct . . . Good
> 12 — 17 correct . . . Excellent
> 18 — 20 correct . . . Exceptional

CHRISTMAS SPIRIT

Top up your Christmas spirit with this measure of seasonal words. Tick the word or phrase you believe is nearest in meaning to the key word. Then turn to the answers to see your score.

wassail — A: dance. B: horn cup. C: toast. D: beer hall.

Christmas disease — A: severe indigestion. B: blood disorder. C: rash caused by holly. D: Christmas season depression.

magi — A: Irish dancing step. B: wise men. C: foreign holiday. D: retirement.

myrrh — A: gum resin. B: Turkish rock. C: costly oil. D: irritating cough.

solstice — A: medieval salt cellar. B: time when the sun stands still. C: Boxing-day pick-me-up. D: six-pointed star.

round robin — A: bird's nest. B: messenger. C: petition. D: steamed pudding.

hoar — A: woodland animal. B: secret store. C: Scrooge-like person. D: white frost.

Yule — A: pine tree. B: celebration. C: icing. D: festival.

manger — A: carpenter's tool-rack. B: feeding trough. C: device for closing stable door. D: haystack.

wattle — A: wooden rattle. B: flickering of Christmas-tree lights. C: family argument. D: part of a turkey.

epiphany — A: donkey's bridle. B: manifestation. C: long letter. D: Oriental herb.

66Many people who have the gift of gab don't know how to wrap it up.**99**

—ARNOLD H. GLASOW

> **66** Do the best you can in every task, no matter how unimportant it may seem at the time. No one learns more about a problem than the person at the bottom. **99**
>
> —SANDRA DAY O'CONNOR

---

deck — A: to gather mistletoe. B: adorn. C: erect scaffolding.
    D: apply veneer.
deciduous — A: decisive. B: refereeing. C: temporary.
    D: low-alcohol.
whim-wham — A: sweet trifle. B: pet rabbit. C: toy.
    D: capricious act.
tinsel — A: sparkling material. B: Cornish mine. C: chocolate coins.
    D: metal garter.
negus — A: rear end of a pantomime horse. B: Spanish wine.
    C: slang for an antiques dealer. D: hot drink.
nativity — A: document proving nationality. B: birth. C: stable.
    D: path of a comet.
tintinnabulation — sound of A: ringing bells. B: ringing in the ears.
    C: rain on windows. D: clashing swords.
convivial — A: persuasive. B: penitent. C: festive.
    D: argumentative.
wintergreen — A: wreath of holly. B: aromatic plant. C: vegetable
    dye. D: mild winter.

> **66** It wasn't that he remembered; it was that he never forgot. **99**
>
> —JAMES GRADY

ANSWERS

wassail — C: A toast, an old-fashioned way of saying, "Bottoms up"; also the drink, usually spiced ale or wine, used for such a toast. Old Norse *ves heill* (be in health).

Christmas disease — B: blood disorder; a disease, similar to haemophilia, found in a man with the surname Christmas and named after him. First reported in the *British Medical Journal* in December 1952.

magi — B: Wise men. The three *magi* or wise men from the East who brought gifts to the infant Jesus (Matt. 2:1); also a member of a priestly class of ancient Persia. Greek *magos*.

myrrh — A: Gum resin, used in perfume or medicine. "The magi brought gold, frankincense and *myrrh*." Greek *murra*.

solstice — B: Either of the times of year—midwinter and midsummer—when the sun is furthest from the equator and seems to stand still. "The winter *solstice* marks the shortest day of the year." Latin *sol* (sun) and *sistere* (to make stand).

round robin — C: a petition on which the signatures appear in a circle so no one person can be identified as the ringleader.

hoar — D: White frost or frozen dew, hoarfrost; also, grey with age. Old English *har* (old, venerable).

Yule — D: Festival, originally heathen, but now applied to Christmas. "On Christmas Eve, the yule log is burnt in the hearth." Old English *geol*.

manger — B: Feeding-trough. "She checked the manger was full of hay before leaving the stable." Old French *mangeoire*.

wattle — D: Part of a turkey: the dangling, fleshy lobe on its throat or head. Sixteenth-century English.

epiphany — B: Manifestation; the twelfth day after Christmas, when the manifestation of Christ to the magi is celebrated. Greek *epiphaneia*.

deck — B: Adorn. "The children *decked* the room with paper chains." Old English.

deciduous — C: Temporary; falling off, like leaves in autumn. "*Deciduous* trees are bare in winter." Latin *de-* (off) and *cadere* (to fall).

whim-wham — C: Toy, plaything. "By Boxing-day, many *whim-whams* have been broken."

tinsel — A: Sparkling material. "The tree glittered with *tinsel.*" Latin *scintilla* (spark).

negus — D: A hot drink of port, sugar, lemon and spices, named after its eighteenth-century inventor, Colonel Frank Negus.

nativity — B: Birth, especially that of Christ. "Each year the nativity is re-enacted in a play." Latin *nasci* (to be born).

tintinnabulation — A: Sound of ringing bells. "The air was filled with *tintinnabulation* from churches across the city." Latin *tintinnabulum* (tinkling bell).

convivial — C: Festive. "The party had a *convivial* atmosphere." Latin *convivium* (feast).

wintergreen — B: Aromatic plant, used for flavouring and in medicine, that remains green in winter. Dutch *wintergroen.*

Vocabulary Ratings

> 9 — 11 correct ... Good
> 12 — 17 correct ... Excellent
> 18 — 20 correct ... Exceptional

❝The real art of conversation is not only to say the right thing in the right place, but to leave unsaid the wrong thing at the tempting moment.**❞**

—Dorothy Nevill

These words are gaining currency or taking on new meanings in the 1990s. Some of them, written or spoken daily, are still too new to appear in standard dictionaries. So vault into the future by picking what you think are the right answers. Then turn the page for your score.

channel surf — A: to sail across rough water. B: switch TV channels. C: sharpen TV images. D: swim between two land formations.

multimedia — A: information overload. B: combination of media. C: news interpretation. D: TV anchor people.

laptop — A: piece of furniture. B: tray. C: portable computer. D: small pet.

leverage — A: to enhance. B: purchase. C: unite. D: compromise.

globalise — A: to equalize. B: anticipate. C: make worldwide. D: initiate.

biogas — fuel from A: decaying organic matter. B: natural-gas wells. C: synthetic oil. D: heavy water.

triple-witching hour — a stock-market period of A: celebration. B: expiration of investment contracts. C: inactivity. D: three price upturns.

megacity — city that is A: large. B: new. C: ancient. D: abandoned.

transnational — A: from coast to coast. B: local switching. C: beyond national boundaries. D: inclusive.

real-time — A: as rapidly as needed. B: local. C: unsyncopated. D: broadcast live.

TRAIT MARKS

Optimists are nostalgic about the future

—QUOTED IN CHICAGO TRIBUNE

Pessimists always take the cynic route

—ANTONI TABAK IN THE WALL STREET JOURNAL

"May you look back on the past with as much pleasure as you look forward to the future."

—PAUL DICKSON, TOASTS (DELACORTE)

---

information superhighway — A: computerised traffic control. B: new school programmes. C: space probes. D: computer communications infrastructure.

fusion reaction — A: detonation. B: meltdown. C: disorder. D: a combining.

on-line — A: financially sound. B: pre-release. C: longitudinal. D: connected.

spin doctor — A: opinion manipulator. B: disc jockey. C: coach. D: forecaster

digital — A: precise. B: clear. C: hand-held. D: using numbers.

aquifer — A: air purifier. B: dust particle. C: tree. D: water-bearing rock.

alternative — A: non-traditional. B: mixed. C: suitable. D: lively.

tabloid — A: freak. B: sensationalist newspaper. C: marble slab. D: statistic.

biotechnology — study of A: planets. B: brain's evolution. C: human communities. D: modification of products.

Internet — A: fabric. B: computer network. C: satellite. D: spy organisation.

channel surf — B: To switch from one TV channel to another in search of a more appealing programme.

multimedia — B: Combination of modes of communication, such as video, audio and text; as, video games using *multimedia*. Latin *multi-* (many) and media.

laptop — C: Portable computer, small enough to be used on one's lap.

leverage — A: To enhance by making maximum use of an asset; as, to *leverage* personal abilities to the limit.

globalise — C: To make worldwide or universal; as, to *globalise* computer technology. Latin *globus* (spherical body, hence the earth).

biogas — A: Gas used as fuel that is a mixture of carbon dioxide and methane from decaying organic matter. Greek *bio-* (life) and gas.

triple-witching hour — B: In stock markets, trading on four Fridays, one each quarter, when three types of contracts expire, sometimes sending markets into wild gyrations.

megacity — A: Very large city; as, *Megacities* of 20 million inhabitants already exist in Asia and Latin America. Greek *mega-* (very large) and city.

transnational — C: Extending beyond the limits, interests or boundaries of a nation; as, *transnational* economic policies. Latin *trans-* (across) and national.

real-time — A: Said of computer calculations: capable of being performed as rapidly as the process or event they describe; as, *Real-time* computing is essential for missile interception.

information superhighway — D: A planned electronic "highway" of 500 channels or more, carrying vast amounts of information and entertainment that will interact with computers and television sets.

fusion reaction — D: The combining of atomic nuclei to form a more massive nucleus while releasing energy. Latin *fundere* (to melt).

on-line — D: Connected to a computer or telecommunications network; available while so linked; as, *on-line* information services.

spin doctor — A: Adroit manipulator of public opinion who takes damaging situations and turns them into something more favourable; as, The *spin doctors* presented the politician's blunder as an amusing incident.

digital — D: Using numbers for display or as the basis for electronic information storage; as, a *digital* watch; *digital* recording technology. Latin *digitus* (finger).

aquifer — D: Underground water-bearing layer of porous rock supplying water for streams, wells and suchlike. Latin *aqua* (water) and *ferre* (to bear, bring, carry).

alternative — A: Designating non-traditional or unconventional choices; as, *alternative* energy sources. Latin *alternare* (to do by turns).

tabloid — B: Newspaper relying heavily on sensationalist headlines and reporting; as, The *tabloids* fuelled the scandal.

biotechnology — D: Use of living organisms or processes to modify or make products and to improve plants or animals; as, The *biotechnology* revolution in agriculture will help feed developing nations.

Internet — B: A huge, mostly unregulated complex of university, government and corporate computer networks.

Vocabulary Ratings
> 9 — 11 correct . . . Good
> 12 — 17 correct . . . Excellent
> 18 — 20 correct . . . Exceptional

Wit Bits

Resume: best feats forward —Bob Thaves

Metrognome:  city elf —Linda Dimit

IN OTHER WORLDS

The daring and adventure of astronauts in space captivate our imaginations. The words in this quiz come from articles in Reader's Digest *about space exploits. Choose the answers you think are correct. Turn the page to check your score.*

asteroid — A: robot. B: space creature. C: tiny planet.
D: black hole.

titanic — A: unforgettable. B: disastrous. C: ancient.
D: gigantic.

composite — A: solid. B: mock-up. C: compound.
D: intricate design.

trajectory — A: flight path. B: take-off. C: long-range forecast.
D: data.

gantry — A: entrance. B: movable structure. C: storage area.
D: timing device.

orientation — A: speed. B: quietness. C: position.
D: flight schedule.

thermal — pertaining to A: daytime. B: night-time.
C: barometric pressure. D: heat.

suborbital — A: underpowered. B: floating in space.
C: without electronics. D: not in orbit.

litany — A: explanation. B: translation. C: repetition.
D: short description.

66The only real voyage of discovery consists not in seeking new landscapes but in having new eyes.**99**

—MARCEL PROUST

" The sun, with all those planets revolving around it and dependent on it, can still ripen a bunch of grapes as if it had nothing else in the universe to do. **"**

—GALILEO

crescent — A: colourful. B: pale. C: shaped in a curve.
D: enfolding.

entrée — A: access. B: lower atmosphere. C: sequence of events.
D: focus.

refract — A: to bend. B: back up. C: scatter. D: reconstruct.

corrugated — A: confirmed. B: wrinkled. C: sifted.
D: arranged in order.

stark — A: brave. B: desolate. C: dangerous. D: unyielding.

dross — A: reflection. B: filament. C: waste matter. D: spacesuit.

quadrant — A: escape mechanism. B: fourth of a circle.
C: gyroscope. D: module's antenna.

microbes — A: pebbles. B: parts of a telescope. C: germs.
D: radio waves.

Perseids — A: cosmic wind. B: Milky Way. C: moons.
D: shooting stars.

heliopause — A: solar system's boundary. B: rocket malfunction.
C: absence of helium. D: halo effect.

flyby — A: aborted mission. B: near miss. C: flight past a
predetermined point. D: annoying fluctuation.

" An age is called Dark, not because the light fails to shine, but because people refuse to see it. **"**

—JAMES A. MICHENER, SPACE (RANDOM HOUSE)

 *ANSWERS*

asteroid — C: One of thousands of tiny planets whose orbits lie mainly between Mars and Jupiter. Greek *aster* (star).

titanic — D: Gigantic; of enormous size, power; as, "Jupiter's *titanic* storms." Greek *Titan* (one of a mythological family of giants).

composite — C: Compound; object made up of various separate parts. Latin *componere* (to put together).

trajectory — A: Flight path; as, "They fired Voyager 2's thrusters for a *trajectory* correction." Latin *traicere* (to throw across).

gantry — B: High movable structure with platforms used to service spacecraft. Old French *gantier* (wooden frame).

orientation — C: Position in relation to the points of the compass; as, "Meanwhile, Voyager 2 is maintaining its own *orientation*." Latin *oriens* (direction of the rising sun).

thermal — D: Pertaining to heat; as, "the giant [rocket] booster, groaning and rumbling with *thermal* tension." Greek *therme* (heat).

suborbital — D: Not in orbit; not completing a full orbit around the earth; as, the "historic *suborbital* lob in 1961." Latin *sub-* (under) and *orbis* (circle, wheel).

litany — C: Any repetitive recital; also, a formal prayer; as, "We read through the familiar *litany* of checklists." Greek *litanos* (pleading).

crescent — C: Shaped in a curve like the moon in its first or last quarter; as, "We could see the *crescent* moon through the spacecraft's windows." Old French *creistre* (to increase).

entrée — A: Access; the right to enter or make use of; as, His past experience gave him *entrée* to the Apollo programme. French, from *entrer* (to enter).

refract — A: Bend a light ray through mediums of different density, such as air and water; as, "a halo of *refracted* sunlight." Latin *refringere* (to break up).

corrugated — B: Wrinkled; formed into parallel ridges or folds; as, the *corrugated* surface. Latin *corrugare* (to wrinkle).

stark — B: Desolate; bleak; as, "The moon was as *stark* as I'd imagined." Also, utter, complete; as, *stark* terror. Old English *stearc* (strong, severe).

dross — C: Waste matter; scum; as, "These meteors are the *dross* of a great comet that began disintegrating thousands of years ago." Old English *dros* (dregs).

quadrant — B: One of the four equal parts of a circle; as, "Meteors appear in every *quadrant* of the sky." Latin *quadrans*.

microbes — C: Germs; microscopic organisms, such as bacteria that cause disease. Greek *mikros* (small) and *bios* (life).

Perseids — D: Shooting stars; annual shower of meteors radiating from the constellation Perseus.

heliopause — A: The boundary or fringe that separates our solar system from outer space. Greek *helios* (sun) and English *pause*.

flyby — C: Flight of a spacecraft or aircraft past a planet or other predetermined point; as, "NASA has scheduled asteroid *flybys* for its Galileo probe." U.S. origin.

Vocabulary Ratings

> 9 — 11 correct ... Good
>
> 12 — 17 correct ... Excellent
>
> 18 — 20 correct ... Exceptional

IF . . .

" . . . those space scientists are so smart, why do they all count backwards? **"**

—ORBEN'S CURRENT COMEDY

OVER THE RAINBOW

Colour words only describe what we see, and some "colourful" words portray emotions and conditions. How many correct answers can you pick from the following array? Turn the page to see how you rate on this verbal colour chart.

verdure — A: blue. B: fragrance. C: green. D: white.

sallow — relating to A: an unhealthy complexion. B: a gaunt look. C: a small valley. D: a facial expression.

rubicund — A: countrified. B: jolly. C: moon-like. D: reddish.

towhead — person with A: an aura. B: light-coloured hair. C: a dull wit. D: a golden crown.

cerulean — A: grey and murky. B: shining. C: engraved in wax. D: sky blue.

roseate — A: ornate. B: delicate. C: thorny. D: optimistic.

hoary — A: rough. B: lewd. C: humorous. D: ancient.

tawny — A: spotted. B: brownish-yellow. C: shaggy. D: light purple.

livid — A: enraged. B: ominous. C: disfigured. D: confused.

emblazon — A: set fire to. B: decorate. C: spread out. D: permit.

iridescent — showing A: joy. B: transparency. C: interplay of colours. D: a temporary situation.

❝Our Creator would never have made such lovely days and have given us the deep hearts to enjoy them unless we were meant to be immortal.**❞**

—NATHANIEL HAWTHORNE

TINT TYPES

Jaded by too much luxury

Azured of a bright future —George O. Ludcke

Plum tuckered out —Bonnie Blaser

---

jaundiced — A: anxious. B: peculiar. C: sad. D: embittered.

swarthy — A: rough and ready. B: hairy. C: pearl grey.
D: dark-complexioned.

tabby — cat that is A: orange with white stripes.
B: black with white spots. C: light-coloured with dark
stripes. D: calico-coloured.

hazel — A: blue-green. B: grey-blue. C: light golden brown.
D: flecked with blue.

harlequin — A: pulsating green. B: yellow-and-black.
C: multicoloured. D: fluorescent orange.

terracotta — A: brownish-red. B: rock-like. C: pale grey.
D: tortoise-shell markings.

ebony — wood that is A: white. B: dark. C: soft. D: pale.

gild — A: cover with gold. B: paint in flat colours.
C: make geometric designs. D: speckle.

monochromatic — A: glistening. B: dull. C: silver.
D: done in one colour.

66Spring is nature's way of saying 'Let's party!'**99**

—ROBIN WILLIAMS

 *ANSWERS*

verdure — C: Green; colour of fresh or new vegetation; as, the *verdure* of spring grass. Old French *verd*.

sallow — A: Relating to an unhealthy yellowish complexion; as, The patient was *sallow* and thin. Old English *salu*.

rubicund — D: Reddish; ruddy; as, the cheerful, *rubicund* face of the farmer. Latin *rubicundus*.

towhead — B: Person with very light-coloured hair. From English *tow* (fibre of flax) and *head*.

cerulean — D: Sky blue; azure; as, The eighteenth-century artist Tiepolo is known for the *cerulean* skies in his paintings. Latin *caelum* (sky, heaven).

roseate — D: Highly optimistic; rosy; as, a *roseate* economic forecast. Latin *roseus* (rosy).

hoary — D: Ancient; venerable; time-honoured; as, a *hoary* myth. Also, white or grey; as the *hoary*-headed prospector. Old English *har* (grey with age).

tawny — B: Brownish-yellow; similar to the colour of tanned leather; as, the *tawny* mane of a lion. Old French *tanner* (to tan).

livid — A: Enraged; angry; as, The insult made him *livid*. Also, black-and-blue; as, a livid mark on the leg. Latin *lividus* (bluish).

emblazon — B: Decorate with bright colours or designs; as, to *emblazon* a poster. Also, to celebrate; as, achievements *emblazoned* in history. English *em-* (into) and *blazon* (shield; coat of arms).

iridescent — C: Showing an interplay of colours resembling a rainbow with shifting hues and patterns; as, an *iridescent* oil slick. Latin *iris* (rainbow).

jaundiced — D: Embittered; resentful; jealous; as, *jaundiced* comments. Latin *galbinus* (greenish-yellowish).

swarthy — D: Dark-complexioned; as, the *swarthy* face of the hunter. Old English *sweart*.

tabby — C: Cat with dark or wavy stripes on a lighter-coloured fur. Also, a silk or wavy appearance. Arabic *al-'attabiya* (the quarter of Baghdad where the silk was made).

hazel — C: Light golden-brown, resembling the hazelnut; as, *hazel* eyes. Middle English *hasel* from Latin *corylus* (hazel shrub).

harlequin — C: Multicoloured; colourful; as, a *harlequin* sweater. From a masked comic character dressed in diamond-patterned tights of many colours. Old French *hierlekin* (demon).

terracotta — A: Brownish-red, from the clay used in *terracotta* pottery, sculpture and the like. Italian (baked earth).

ebony — B: Dark, heavy hardwood of various tropical trees of Asia and Africa. Greek *ebenos*.

gild — A: Cover with a thin layer of gold. Also, to make something seem better than it is; as, to *gild* a mistake. Old English *gyldan*.

monochromatic — D: Done in one colour or different shades of one colour; as, *monochromatic* paintings. Greek *monos* (single) and *chroma* (colour).

Vocabulary Ratings
> 9 — 11 correct ... Good
> 12 — 17 correct ... Excellent
> 18 — 20 correct ... Exceptional

❝People from a planet without flowers would think we must be mad with joy the whole time to have such things about us.**❞**

—Iris Murdoch, A Fairly Honourable Defeat
(Viking Penguin)

HEAVEN AND EARTH

Many of our words have their roots both on Earth and in the heavens. How many of these hybrids do you recognise? Turn the page for your score.

jovial — A: merry. B: laid-back. C: pleasingly plump. D: ruddy.

pedigree — A: study of children. B: diploma. C: ancestral line. D: stamp of approval.

homogeneous — A: relating to humans. B: similar. C: melancholy. D: cheerful and upbeat.

sleuth — A: timidity. B: detective. C: carelessness. D: opening in a dam.

aftermath — A: result. B: critique. C: concise summary. D: type of appendix.

cocksure — A: cynical. B: angry. C: insensitive and uncaring. D: overly confident.

nausea — A: despair. B: uncertainty. C: sickness in the stomach. D: indifference.

canard — A: ominous warning. B: malicious rumour. C: humorous proverb. D: small bucket.

ruminate — A: become nostalgic. B: wander about. C: ponder. D: search for.

cordial — A: happy. B: perceptive. C: friendly. D: sophisticated.

66Love beauty; it is the shadow of God on the universe.**99**

—GABRIELA MISTRAL, DESOLACIÓN (HISPANIC INSTITUTE)

HAIKU

Day slipped the sun in
an envelope of clouds; night
sealed it with a star.

—*JOYCE B. ANDREWS*

---

reek — A: throw into disorder. B: be soaking wet.
C: take revenge. D: give off an unpleasant odour.

solar plexus — area of the A: abdomen. B: head. C: back.
D: chest.

germinate — A: begin to grow. B: be relevant. C: be creative.
D: stimulate.

ferret — A: search out. B: camouflage. C: plunder.
D: move quickly.

dog days — period of A: being carefree. B: having youthful flings.
C: misfortune. D: hot weather.

wheedle — A: shout. B: coax. C: pry. D: lie to.

fathom — A: understand. B: explain. C: decide. D: reach out.

halcyon — A: shimmering. B: pertaining to the air we breathe.
C: fresh and bracing. D: calm and peaceful.

wisp — A: brief glance. B: hush. C: speech defect.
D: something slight.

oval — shaped like A: an apple. B: a banana. C: an egg.
D: a rhomboid.

YAWNING OF A NEW DAY

The darkness came unstuck from the seam where
lake and sky meet.

—*LARRY WEINTRAUB IN CHICAGO SUN-TIMES*

Dawn crept in tie-dyed majesty through the shadows.

—*PETER HATHAWAY CAPSTICK*

jovial — A: Merry; having a playful, hearty good humour. From the planet Jupiter, considered by astrologers to be a happy influence.

pedigree — C: Ancestral line; family tree. Middle French *pié de grue* (crane's foot, which resembles the lines of descent in genealogical charts).

homogeneous — B: Similar; alike; of the same nature; as, Our townspeople are too *homogeneous*; we miss the diverse population of the cities. Greek *homogenes*.

sleuth — B: Detective. Shortened form of sleuthhound, a bloodhound that tracks a trail by scent. Old Norse *sloth* (track, trail).

aftermath — A: Result or consequence; as, The picnic had an unfortunate *aftermath*; we got poison ivy. Also, grass that grows after mowing. Old English *math* (mowing).

cocksure — D: Overly confident; absolutely certain. From *cock* (rooster, notable for his confident strutting) and *sure*.

nausea — C: A feeling of sickness in the stomach; as, He had *nausea* from the rolling and pitching of the ship. Latin, from Greek *naus* (ship).

canard — B: Malicious rumour; false report. French (duck; hoax). From *vendre un canard à moitié* (to pretend to sell a duck; cheat).

ruminate — C: Ponder; turn over and over in the mind; as, The wise old man *ruminated* on my question. Latin *ruminare* (to chew one's cud as a cow—a ruminant—does).

cordial — C: Friendly; warm and sincere; gracious; as, Her *cordial* welcome made everyone feel at ease. Latin *cor* (heart).

reek — D: Give off an unpleasant odour; as, When accused by a woman of smelling, the incomparable Samuel Johnson is said to have replied, "Nay, madam. You smell. I *reek*." Old English *reocan*.

solar plexus — A: Area of the abdomen having an interlacing of nerves that radiate like rays of the sun. Latin *sol* (sun) and *plexus* (braid; network).

germinate — A: Begin to grow or develop; as, Meetings *germinate* ideas; seeds *germinate* into plants. Latin *germinare* (to sprout).

ferret — A: Search or find out by persistent investigation; as, to *ferret* out facts the way a ferret (a small weasel-like animal) drives rabbits from burrows.

dog days — D: Hot, sultry weather during July and August, so called because Sirius the Dog Star rises and sets with the sun.

wheedle — B: Coax; persuade by flattery; as, The teenager *wheedled* use of the convertible out of his father. Perhaps from German *wedeln* (to wag the tail).

fathom — A: Understand; get to the bottom of; as, She couldn't *fathom* his motive. From *fathom*, a six-foot-long measure of water's depth. Old English *faethm* (outstretched arms).

halcyon — D: Calm, peaceful and idyllic. Greek *alkyon*, a mythological bird that calmed wind and waves during the winter solstice.

wisp — D: Something slight or delicate, such as a streak of smoke or lock of hair; as, a *wisp* of a girl. Middle English.

oval — C: Having the shape of the long cross-section of an egg. Latin *ovum* (egg).

Vocabulary Ratings

> 9 — 11 correct . . . Good
> 12 — 17 correct . . . Excellent
> 18 — 20 correct . . . Exceptional

ONE WORLD

Many words in the news relate to the preservation and restoration of the environment. How many of the following words do you recognise? Turn the page to find out your verbal ecological score.

sediment — A: particles in a liquid. B: noble feeling. C: cast-off material. D: shallow-rooted organism.

porous — A: fragile. B: opaque. C: malleable. D: full of tiny holes.

acid rain — A: polluted precipitation. B: mist from a geyser. C: vegetation emission. D: nuclear fallout.

jetty — A: spurt of water. B: conduit. C: breakwater. D: sandy shoal.

sirocco — A: seasonal South Asian cyclone. B: Pacific hurricane. C: Alpine snowstorm. D: hot African wind.

tundra — plain in A: South America. B: Africa. C: India. D: arctic regions.

radon — A: laser beam. B: radioactive gas. C: detection system. D: solar-heat collector.

greenhouse effect — A: gardening method. B: algae in lakes. C: global warming of earth. D: increased fertility.

estuary — A: waterfall. B: silt deposit. C: junction of two rivers. D: mouth of a river.

atmospheric inversion — A: drought condition. B: jet-stream shift. C: reversal of thermal conditions. D: cause of tropical storm.

❝The two most powerful warriors are patience and time.❞

—*LEO TOLSTOY*

TAKING A BOUGH

Trees playing "London Bridge" with an old country road.

—Marilyn Wolfe

Old trees sticking their knobby toes out of the sidewalk.

—Colleen McCullough

---

spit — A: outcropping of rock. B: peak. C: point of land.
D: fissure.

pristine — A: strict. B: exacting. C: unspoiled. D: shimmering.

ozone — A: engine's exhaust. B: form of oxygen.
C: nature's heat retainer. D: gas in spray cans.

potable — A: movable. B: drinkable. C: strong. D: clear.

habitat — A: native environment. B: outer covering.
C: usual routine. D: historical information.

mutation — A: a silencing. B: irreparable damage. C: change.
D: disorder.

defoliant — A: odour suppressant. B: poisonous weed.
C: powerful fungicide. D: leaf-stripping substance.

herbicide — A: weed killer. B: decorative container.
C: plant blight. D: herb garden.

moraine — A: crest of hill. B: shallow lake. C: mountain valley.
D: glacial deposit.

toxic — A: poisonous. B: long-lasting. C: bad-smelling.
D: unsanitary.

66The sky is the daily bread of the eyes.**99**

—*RALPH WALDO EMERSON*

 *ANSWERS*

sediment — A: Fine particles of foreign matter in a liquid; as, *sediment* in drinking water. Also, sand, silt or gravel laid down by wind or water. Latin *sedere* (to sit or settle).

porous — D: Full of tiny holes that allow liquid or air to pass through; absorbent; as, *Porous* sandstone stores water. Latin *porus* (an opening).

acid rain — A: Rain or snow polluted with acids released by exhaust from factories and by burning fossil fuels such as coal.

jetty — C: Breakwater; as, a pile of rocks extending into the water from the shore to protect harbours. Old French *jeter* (to throw).

sirocco — D: Hot spring wind from northern Africa that blows across the Mediterranean to southern Europe. Arabic *sharq* (the rising of the sun).

tundra — D: Rolling, treeless plain of the arctic regions. Russian, from Lapp *tundar* (bare hill).

radon — B: Radioactive gas formed from the decay of radium in the earth; as, Homes affected by *radon* can be made safe.

greenhouse effect — C: Global warming of the earth. Carbon dioxide in the atmosphere prevents some of the sun's heat from escaping earth (similar to the way heat is retained in a greenhouse).

estuary — D: Mouth of a river where it mixes with the sea; as, Coastal waters and *estuaries* are in crisis from pollution. Latin *aestus* (tide).

atmospheric inversion — C: Reversal of normal thermal conditions, as occurs when warmer air prevents cooler, denser surface air from rising. Pollutants can become trapped in the cool air.

spit — C: Narrow point of land or shoal projecting into the water. Old English *spitu*.

pristine — C: Unspoiled; pure and untouched; primitive; as, the *pristine* snow that blankets the highest peaks of the mountains. Latin *pristinus* (former).

ozone — B: Form of oxygen that is created in the upper atmosphere and that protects life from harmful ultraviolet radiation; as, the worldwide *ozone* shield. Greek *ozein* (to smell).

potable — B: Drinkable; suitable for drinking; as, The town's water supply was no longer *potable*. Latin *potare* (to drink).

habitat — A: The native or natural environment of an animal or plant; as, the necessity of preserving vital waterfowl *habitats*. Latin (it inhabits).

mutation — C: Change in form, structure or function in an organism caused by a genetic alteration. Latin *mutare* (to change).

defoliant — D: Substance sprayed on plants to strip growing plants of their leaves. Latin *de-* (away) and *folium* (leaf).

herbicide — A: A chemical that is used to kill weeds, grass or brush. Latin *herba* (herb, grass) and *-cida* (killer of).

moraine — D: Rocks, gravel, sand and clay deposited by a glacier; as, Certain *moraines* may dam streams to form lakes. French, from dialectal *morêna* (mound of earth).

toxic — A: Poisonous; as, a toxic dump. Greek *toxikon* (poison used on arrow tips).

Vocabulary Ratings
    9 — 11 correct . . . Good
    12 — 17 correct . . . Excellent
    18 — 20 correct . . . Exceptional

"The world is so empty if one thinks only of mountains, rivers and cities; but to know someone who thinks and feels with us, and who, though distant is close to us in spirit, this makes the earth for us an inhabited garden.**"**

—*GOETHE*

NATURE'S HEALING TOUCH

"We should pay attention to the ways of nature and learn to encourage the body's own innate mechanisms of self-repair," writes Dr. Andrew Weil in the Reader's Digest Family Guide to Natural Medicine. *Words in the following quiz are drawn from this book. Check the answers you believe are correct, then turn the page to check your score.*

aerobic exercise — activity related to A: meditation.
B: oxygen consumption. C: yoga. D: inflammation control.

prevalent — A: infectious. B: widespread. C: self-evident.
D: incurable.

avid — A: undisciplined. B: stingy. C: eager. D: belligerent.

succumb — A: fail. B: give in. C: continue. D: keep under control.

botanicals — A: fossil remnants. B: health foods. C: cosmetic
products. D: medications made from plants.

placebo — A: familiar nostrum. B: quiet place. C: unmedicated substance. D: sleeping pill.

orthodox — A: conventional. B: precise. C: rigid. D: skeletal.

homeopathy — treatment with A: home remedies.
B: small doses of medicine. C: sea water. D: biofeedback.

mandala — A: historic medical text. B: instrument. C: chant.
D: symbolic design.

holistic medicine — treatment emphasising A: relaxation.
B: mind control. C: the whole person. D: holiness.

proponent — A: advocate. B: opponent. C: interpreter.
D: specialist.

LIKE IT IS

Life expectancy would grow by leaps and bounds if green
vegetables smelled as good as bacon.

—DOUG LARSON, UNITED FEATURE SYNDICATE

AGAINST THE GRAIN
Viewing nature in the raw
Once made me feel ethereal,
But I lost my sense of awe
When it wound up as my cereal.

—*MERRY BROWNE*

---

antibody — A: bacterium. B: multivitamin. C: protective protein.
D: clotting substance.

placate — A: pacify. B: compensate. C: be aware of.
D: conceive of.

itinerant — A: occasional. B: sickly. C: travelling. D: temporary.

acupuncture — medical practice concerned with A: relieving pain.
B: building muscle strength. C: draining an abscess.
D: lowering cholesterol.

complement — A: flatter. B: make complete. C: duplicate.
D: enlarge.

therapeutic — A: natural. B: curative. C: reinforcing.
D: energising.

microcosm — A: well-ordered system. B: study of microbes.
C: power of microscopes. D: miniature representation.

t'ai chi — A: faith and belief. B: life energy. C: massage to music.
D: system of exercises.

postulate — A: claim. B: question. C: lie. D: be uncritical.

 *ANSWERS*

aerobic exercise — B: Running, dancing, swimming or other activity that improves the body's oxygen consumption. Greek *aer* (air) and *bios* (life).

prevalent — B: Widespread; commonly occurring; as, "illnesses *prevalent* in an ageing population." Latin *praevalere* (to be strong).

avid — C: Eager and enthusiastic; as, "An *avid* experimenter, he began to test remedies on himself." Latin *avere* (to desire).

succumb — B: Give in to an overwhelming desire or force; as, "Why do some people *succumb* and others do not?" Latin *succumbere* (lie down under).

botanicals — D: Medications made from plants; as, Chinese practitioners of herbal medicine use *botanicals*. Greek *botane* (plant).

placebo — C: Unmedicated substance or harmless pill; as, The volunteers were given the experimental drug, while the control group received a *placebo*. Latin (I shall please).

orthodox — A: Holding conventional, conservative or currently accepted beliefs; as, *orthodox* medicine. Greek *orthodoxos* (right opinion).

homeopathy — B: Treatment of disease by medicine given in minute doses that in healthy people normally produce symptoms of that disease. Greek *homöopathie* (likeness of feeling).

mandala — D: Symbolic design in Hinduism or Buddhism that represents the universe or wholeness. Often used in meditation. Sanskrit (circle).

holistic medicine — C: Treatment emphasising "the whole person—body and mind—as opposed to focusing only on the part of the body where symptoms occur." Greek *holos* (whole).

proponent — A: Advocate; person who supports a cause or makes a proposal; as, "According to *proponents*, [such] training teaches better use of the body." Latin *proponere* (to put forth).

antibody — C: Protective protein in the blood that attempts to immunise the body against specific illness-causing substances; as, Mother's milk contains *antibodies* to protect newborns. Translation of German *Antikörper*.

placate — A: Pacify; appease; as, "Shamanic societies attribute ill-defined illnesses to spirits who must be *placated*." Latin *placare* (to calm).

itinerant — C: Travelling from place to place, usually to do work; as, Andrew Still, a conventionally trained *itinerant* physician, founded osteopathy. Latin *itinerari* (to travel).

acupuncture — A: Method of relieving pain or treating illness by inserting needles in specific parts of the body. Latin *acus* (needle).

complement — B: Make complete; form a whole with another part; as, "Homeopathic medicines may be used to *complement* conventional medical treatment." Latin *complere*.

therapeutic — B: Curative; having healing qualities; as, The doctor outlined a *therapeutic* diet. Greek *therapeuein* (to treat medically).

microcosm — D: Miniature representation of a larger system; as, "The human body is seen as a *microcosm* of the universe." Greek *mikros kosmos* (little world).

t'ai chi — D: System of physical exercises, developed in China, for self-defence and meditation. Chinese *t'ai chi ch'uan* (extreme limit boxing).

postulate — A: Claim; assume to be true; as, "Another theory *postulates* that the treatment relaxes the body." Latin *postulare* (to demand, assert).

Vocabulary Ratings

9 — 11 correct ... Good

12 — 17 correct ... Excellent

18 — 20 correct ... Exceptional

THOUGHT FOR FOOD

Food labels change in look and content due to regulations intended for consumer protection. Knowledge of such terms as those listed below can help you to be better informed when you shop and to eat more healthy foods. Take this test, then turn the page to see if your vocabulary needs enrichment.

organic — A: natural. B: synthetic. C: careful. D: toxic.

nutrient — A: calorie. B: medicine. C: nourishing food. D: mixture.

tofu — A: oriental spice. B: flavouring. C: soybean product.
D: cooking procedure.

cholesterol — A: poison. B: fat. C: muscle strength. D: nerves.

vitamin — A: essential substance. B: mineral. C: digestive aid.
D: pep pill.

megadose — amount or portion that is A: dispensed intermittently.
B: large. C: given once. D: generally prescribed.

carbohydrate — a compound A: produced by plants.
B: made artificially. C: high in protein. D: without water.

beta-carotene — source of A: vitamin A. B: chlorophyll.
C: calcium. D: sugar.

ascorbic acid — A: thiamine. B: bioflavonoid. C: vitamin B-6.
D: vitamin C.

metabolism — A: bacterial growth. B: antibody production.
C: homogenisation. D: conversion of food into energy.

monosodium glutamate — A: smart drug. B: preservative.
C: flavour intensifier. D: emulsifier.

"Those who think they have not time for bodily exercise
will sooner or later have to find time for illness.**"**

—Edward Stanley

Health-food store: "Get on the bran wagon."

—*Quoted by R. Giblin*

Barbecue restaurant: "We will serve no swine before its time."

—*Margaret A. Dierdorff*

Pizza stand: "Another one bites the crust."

—*Quoted by Charlene Black*

---

endorphin — A: deep-sea fish. B: sprouting seed.
   C: a unit of measurement. D: natural painkiller.

collagen — A: swelling. B: weak spot. C: protein. D: deposit of fat.

serotonin — A: cholesterol-reducing substance. B: chemical.
   C: artificial sweetener. D: herbal tea.

gustatory — pertaining to A: taste. B: overeating. C: sourness.
   D: spicy food.

amino acids — A: food preservatives. B: pesticides.
   C: protein "building blocks." D: cleansing solutions.

fructose — A: colouring. B: fruit sugar. C: liquid diet.
   D: soybean milk.

gastronomic — having to do with A: stomach acid. B: a medical
   procedure. C: eating well. D: inexpensive food.

polyunsaturated — with fat content that is A: high. B: medium.
   C: nonexistent. D: low.

sodium chloride — A: table salt. B: bubbly drink. C: baking soda.
   D: antacid.

SIZE CRACK

Extra calories we consume quickly become a *fat accompli.*

—*A. H. Berzen*

 **ANSWERS**

organic — A: Natural; as, *Organic* farming doesn't rely on pesticides or artificial fertilisers. Greek *organikos* (bodily organ).

nutrient — C: Nourishing food that sustains plants and animals; as, Broccoli is *nutrient*-packed. Latin *nutrire* (to nourish).

tofu — C: Soybean product (bean curd) that is a good, no-cholesterol source of protein; as, *Tofu* resembles a soft, white, cheese-like food.

cholesterol — B: Fat-related substance necessary for health; as, Too much *cholesterol* is associated with heart disease.

vitamin — A: Organic substance found in many foods and essential for normal functioning of the body; as, *vitamin* B-6 from meats, whole grains, nuts, etc. Coined by Polish biochemist Casimir Funk in 1911.

megadose — B: Large dose of a drug, medicine or vitamin; as, Any *megadose* should be taken only under a doctor's supervision. Greek *megas* (great) and English *dose*.

carbohydrate — A: A plant-produced compound—such as sugars (honey or cane), starches (rice, corn, wheat or potatoes) and celluloses (skins of fruits, vegetables).

beta-carotene — A: Substance found in such foods as carrots, tomatoes, and broccoli, from which the body produces vitamin A.

ascorbic acid — D: Vitamin C, found in citrus fruits and various vegetables. Greek *a-* (not) and Medieval Latin *scorbutus* (scurvy).

metabolism — D: Process by which the body converts food into energy. Greek *metabole* (change).

monosodium glutamate — C: Flavor intensifier, known also as MSG. In some people, it causes an allergic reaction.

endorphin — D: Natural painkiller made by the brain, with effects similar to those of opium-based drugs, such as morphine.

collagen — C: The fibrous protein that helps hold cells and tissue together.

serotonin — B: Chemical found in the brain and blood that acts as a natural tranquilliser. It is stimulated by eating carbohydrates.

gustatory — A: Pertaining to taste; as, The lasagna proved a *gustatory* delight. Latin *gustare* (to taste).

amino acids — C: Twenty or so organic compounds that are the "building blocks" of protein.

fructose — B: Sugar that occurs naturally in fruit; as, Like sucrose (table sugar), *fructose* supplies empty calories along with sweetening. Latin *fructus* (fruit).

gastronomic — C: Having to do with eating well; as, cuisine planned with *gastronomic* care.

polyunsaturated — D: Describing fats or oils low in saturated fat and not primarily associated with cholesterol formation.

sodium chloride — A: Table salt; as, Doctors may restrict *sodium chloride* intake in heart-disease patients.

Vocabulary Ratings
        9 — 11 correct . . . Good
        12 — 17 correct . . . Excellent
        18 — 20 correct . . . Exceptional

KITCHIONARY

Pesto: someone who keeps bothering an Italian chef

Antipasto: people who don't like Italian cooking

Mince: walk around the kitchen in short, rapid steps

—*QUOTED BY RAY ORROCK IN THE ARGUS*

As you unwrap the "gift" words below, tuck the new ones into your vocabulary box. They come with a lifetime guarantee of satisfaction, and they can add sparkle and power to the way you think and speak. Turn the page to find your score.

swashbuckling — A: daring. B: idealistic. C: drably dressed. D: romantic.

competent — A: agreeable. B: inept. C: vigorous. D: capable.

spritz — A: boat's sail. B: bubble. C: squirt. D: overhanging rock.

omnibus — A: threatening. B: all-embracing. C: round and full. D: slow-moving.

ingenuity — A: innocence. B: cleverness. C: appeal. D: deceitfulness.

canon — A: barrier. B: noisy gathering. C: guiding principle. D: bishop.

parlance — A: gossip. B: small family room. C: witticism. D: manner of speaking.

muster — A: assemble. B: relieve. C: challenge. D: spread around.

personable — A: intimate. B: cheerful. C: attractive. D: superficial.

concave — A: curving outwards. B: oval-shaped. C: collapsing. D: curving inwards.

infatuation — A: sense of security. B: aversion. C: temporary passion. D: feeling of superiority.

66From what we get, we can make a living; what we give, however, makes a life.**99**

—ARTHUR ASHE, DAYS OF GRACE (KNOPF)

66Who does not thank for little will not
thank for much.**99**

—*ESTONIAN PROVERB*

forfeit — A: exchange. B: give up something. C: shield
from harm. D: pull back.

query — A: question. B: look over thoroughly. C: follow through.
D: act peculiarly.

intergalactic — A: extremely fast. B: subatomic. C: radioactive.
D: between star systems.

steadfast — A: slow but sure. B: strong. C: friendly.
D: unwavering.

permutation — A: alteration. B: permission. C: stable combination.
D: seepage.

rookery — A: gambling spot. B: children's playground.
C: animal breeding place. D: camping area.

ransack — A: run wild. B: destroy completely.
C: do things haphazardly. D: search thoroughly.

infamous — A: somewhat annoying. B: unknown.
C: simple and unassuming. D: having a bad reputation.

inkling — A: blemish. B: small object. C: slight indication.
D: assumption.

66Always try to be a little kinder than is necessary.**99**

—*JAMES M. BARRIE*

 *ANSWERS*

swashbuckling — A: Recklessly daring; daredevilish; swaggering; as, an old Errol Flynn *swashbuckling* film about pirates. English *swash* (splashing water) and *buckler* (shield).

competent — D: Capable; well-qualified; as, A *competent* mechanic is a blessing. Latin *competere* (to be suitable).

spritz — C: Squirt or spray; as, A quick *spritz* of this or that will not eliminate termites. German *spritzen* (to spray).

omnibus — B: All-embracing; covering many items; as, The *omnibus* ticket included transportation, accommodation and meals. Latin (for all).

ingenuity — B: Cleverness; inventive skill; resourcefulness; as, the cat's *ingenuity* in opening the refrigerator door. Latin *ingeniosus* (gifted with genius).

canon — C: Guiding principle used as a standard; as, *canons* of good taste. Also, sacred writings of the Bible. Greek *kanon* (measuring rod).

parlance — D: Manner or style of speaking or writing; as, legal *parlance*; my grandmother's quaint *parlance*. Old French *parler* (to speak).

muster — A: Assemble or bring together; summon up; as, to muster troops for inspection; muster courage. Latin *monstrare* (to show).

personable — C: Attractive; having a pleasing manner; as, a *personable* salesclerk. Latin *persona* (person, character).

concave — D: Curving inwards; as, the interesting *concave* shape of an antique bottle. Latin *concavus* (hollow).

infatuation — C: Temporary, unreasoning and shallow passion; as, a teenager's *infatuation* with a rock star. Latin *infatuare* (to make foolish).

forfeit — B: Forced to give up something; to be penalised for wrongdoing. Middle English *forfet* (crime).

query — A: Question; express doubts as to correctness; as, to *query* a company's claim about the benefits of a product. Latin *quaerere* (to ask).

intergalactic — D: Occurring or existing between galaxies; as, *intergalactic* travel in science fiction. Latin *inter-* (between) and English *galactic*, from Greek *galaktikos* (milky; derivation for Milky Way).

steadfast — D: Unwavering; as, a *steadfast* gaze. Also loyal and constant; as, a *steadfast* friend. Old English *stedefaest*.

permutation — A: Alteration or change; complete rearrangement; as, political *permutations* in Eastern Europe. Latin *per-* (through) and *mutare* (to change).

rookery — C: Breeding place of birds, seals or other animals; as, a *rookery* teeming with penguins. English *rook* (black European crow).

ransack — D: Search thoroughly and vigorously; as, to *ransack* a room for a document; also, to plunder. Old Norse *rann* (house) and -*saka* (to search).

infamous — D: Having a bad reputation; notorious; as, No nation can trust that *infamous* dictator. Latin *in* (not) and *fama* (fame).

inkling — C: Slight indication; hint; intimation; as, She had no *inkling* of his true intentions. Middle English *inclen* (to hint).

Vocabulary Ratings
9 — 11 correct . . . Good
12 — 17 correct . . . Excellent
18 — 20 correct . . . Exceptional

66 An informal survey shows that what most people want for Christmas is two more weeks to prepare for it. **99**

—*Bob Stanley in Columbus, Wis., Journal-Republican*

TIME FLIES

Clock your score with the following words, all relating to the theme of time. Tick the word or phrase you believe is nearest in meaning to the key word. Then turn the page for your score.

aboriginal — A: isolated. B: earliest. C: numerous. D: forgotten.

postpone — A: send away. B: cancel. C: appoint.
D: put off.

concur — A: overcome. B: take over. C: agree. D: negotiate.

subsequent — A: following. B: disruptive. C: trivial.
D: dependent.

tardy — A: timely. B: late. C: misplaced. D: careless.

antediluvian — A: very old-fashioned. B: resistant to evil.
C: guaranteed to function. D: going backwards.

momentary — A: important. B: memorable. C: forceful.
D: short-lived.

continual — A: equal. B: unavoidable. C: repetitive. D: restricted.

aeon — A: interval. B: period in history. C: eternity. D: long journey.

medieval — A: according to myth. B: of the Middle Ages.
C: un-sophisticated. D: from the southern hemisphere.

protracted — A: prolonged. B: out of date. C: sentimental.
D: hesitant.

66Not the fastest horse can catch a word
spoken in anger.**99**

—CHINESE PROVERB

> **66**I think God's going to come down and pull civilisation over for speeding.**99**
>
> *—Steven Wright*

---

synchronise — A: identify origin. B: time together. C: estimate age.
   D: make a copy.

current — A: shortened. B: convenient. C: seasonal.
   D: present-day.

epoch — A: part of a story. B: series of events. C: point in time.
   D: prophecy.

punctual — A: prompt. B: predictable. C: fussy. D: hasty.

anachronism — A: unexpected happening. B: coincidence.
   C: error in time. D: ambition.

obsolete — A: immovable. B: enduring. C: premature.
   D: antiquated.

extemporise — A: perform unrehearsed. B: put an end to.
   C: predict. D: underestimate risk.

ultimate — A: everlasting. B: perfect. C: universal. D: final.

retrospect — A: looking back. B: exhibition. C: lengthy speech.
   D: misfortune.

> **66**Sincerity and competence is a strong combination. In politics, it's everything.**99**
>
> *—Peggy Noonan, in Catholic New York*

 *ANSWERS*

aboriginal — B: Earliest; primitive; as, the *aboriginal* population of Australia. Latin *ab origine* (from the beginning).

postpone — D: Put off, delay to a future time. "The football match was *postponed* until the following Wednesday." Latin *post-* (after) and *ponere* (to put).

concur — C: Agree; to act or occur at the same time. "The organisers *concurred* on their arrangements." Latin *con-* (together) and *currere* (to run).

subsequent — A: Following. "The couple met on that day and on many *subsequent* occasions." Latin *sub-* (close to) and *sequi* (to follow).

tardy — B: Late. "He apologised for his *tardy* arrival." Latin *tardus* (slow).

antediluvian — A: Very old-fashioned. Literally, dating from before Noah's Flood. "Students were outraged at the speaker's *antediluvian* ideas." Latin *ante-* (before) and *diluvium* (flood).

momentary — D: Short-lived; temporary. "Her fame was *momentary.*" Latin *momentum* (movement).

continual — C: Repetitive; recurring regularly and frequently; as, *continual* interruptions. Latin *continuare* (to continue).

aeon — C: Eternity; an immeasurably long time. "The history of human civilisation is but a moment in the *aeon* of Creation." Greek *aion*.

medieval — B: Of the Middle Ages—between the fifth-century fall of the Roman Empire and the fifteenth-century Renaissance. "The *medieval* city lay in ruins." Latin *medius* (middle) and *aevum* (age).

protracted — A: Prolonged; drawn out in time. "The deal was completed only after *protracted* negotiations." Latin *pro-* (forth) and *trahere* (to draw).

synchronise — B: Time together; cause to coincide in time. "Celebrations were *synchronised* to start simultaneously around the country." Greek *syn-* (together) and *khronos* (time).

current — D: Present-day; happening now; as, a *current* affairs programme. Latin *currere*.

epoch — C: Point in time beginning a new period; a milestone. Also, an era. "The discovery of antibiotics marked an *epoch* in medical history." Greek *epi-* (upon) and *ekhein* (to hold).

punctual — A: Prompt; on time. "Applicant should be *punctual* for interviews." Latin *punctum* (a point).

anachronism — C: Error in time; placing a person or event in the wrong period. "The clock in Shakespeare's play *Julius Caesar* is an *anachronism*, striking hours 1,300 years before clockwork came into use." Greek *ana-* (backwards) and *khronos*.

obsolete — D: Antiquated; no longer used. "It is predicted that printed books will in time become *obsolete*." Latin *ob-* (because of) and *solere* (to be in the habit).

extemporise — A: Speak unrehearsed, without notes; perform without preparation. "The politician was skilled at *extemporising*." Latin *ex-* (out of) and *tempus* (time).

ultimate — D: Final; most important. "Safety was the *ultimate* consideration." Latin *ultimus* (last).

retrospect — A: Looking back in time. "In *retrospect*, her schooldays seemed happier." Latin *retro-* (backwards) and *specere* (to look).

Vocabulary Ratings
> 9 — 11 correct . . . Good
> 12 — 17 correct . . . Excellent
> 18 — 20 correct . . . Exceptional

CITY LIKES

Tokyo's pace is like a VCR on permanent fast-forward.

—Grania Davis

PUBLIC ADDRESS

The language of government officials at press conferences and public appearances provides us with this list of

test words. How many of them can you correctly define? Turn the page for the answers.

agenda — A: schedule. B: assignment. C: addition.
   D: common practice.

annex — A: destroy. B: add to. C: interpret. D: cross out.

defray — A: use together. B: pull back. C: provide money for.
   D: cheat.

dictate — A: explain. B: defend. C: understand. D: require.

renegade — A: traitorous. B: destitute. C: cowardly.
   D: uncontrollable.

humanitarian — A: patriotic. B: philanthropic. C: common.
   D: misanthropic.

unwarranted — A: non-aggressive. B: unexpected.
   C: disenchanted. D: not justifiable.

modality — A: form or pattern. B: transition. C: difficulty.
   D: experiment.

logistics — A: new concepts. B: game theory. C: organisation
   of supplies. D: normality.

base — A: substantial. B: contemptible. C: reasonable.
   D: average.

66When they call the roll in the Senate, the senators do

not know whether to answer 'Present'

or 'Not guilty.'99

—*THEODORE ROOSEVELT*

> **66** Governing a large country is like frying a small fish.
> You spoil it with too much poking. **99**
>
> —LAO-TSE

profiteer — A: harass. B: make excess profits. C: predict.
D: compete.

implement — A: pry open. B: put into effect. C: penetrate.
D: lead or direct.

transitory — A: unimportant. B: imperfect. C: temporary.
D: fragile.

flag — A: be enthusiastic. B: lose strength. C: punish.
D: challenge.

interdiction — A: decree forbidding something. B: firmness.
C: accusation of wrongdoing. D: plea for leniency.

format — A: adherence to standards. B: repetition.
C: explanation. D: structure or arrangement.

extraneous — A: inconspicuous. B: noticeable. C: unusual.
D: irrelevant.

sequester — A: follow. B: round up. C: withdraw.
D: question closely.

mediator — person who A: intrudes. B: settles disputes.
C: is thoughtful. D: makes demands.

resolute — A: determined. B: blunt. C: opinionated. D: cruel.

> **66** All growth, including political growth, is
> the result of risk-taking. **99**
>
> —JUDE WANNISKI, QUOTED IN THE WALL STREET JOURNAL

 *ANSWERS*

agenda — A: Schedule; list of things to do, especially for a meeting; as, an *agenda* for trade negotiations. Latin.

annex — B: Add to; take by force; incorporate the territory of one country, state or municipality into another; as, the town *annexed* the property for a park. Latin *annexus* (joined).

defray — C: Provide money for expenses; as, Contributions from various sources help *defray* the cost of maintaining bridges. Old French *defraier*.

dictate — D: Require; have need of; as, Additional policy-making sessions will be held as circumstances *dictate*. Latin *dictare* (to say repeatedly).

renegade — A: Traitorous; deserting one cause for another; as, A *renegade* group broke up the rally. Latin *renegare* (to deny).

humanitarian — B: Philanthropic; benevolent; concerned with eliminating suffering; as, a *humanitarian* effort to help the homeless. Latin *humanus* (human).

unwarranted — D: Not justifiable; uncalled for; as, *unwarranted* criticism. English *un-* (not) and Old French *garantir* (to guarantee).

modality — A: Form; conformity to a pattern; as, Recent events necessitate new *modalities* in foreign policy. Latin *modus* (manner).

logistics — C: Organisation of supplies, transporting troops and the like, for a military operation. Greek *logistikos* (skilled in calculation).

base — B: Contemptible; mean-spirited; dishonourable; as, the *base* treatment of refugees. Latin *bassus* (low).

profiteer — B: Make excess profits, particularly by exploiting a shortage of goods. Latin *proficere* (to gain).

implement — B: Put into effect; accomplish; fulfil; as, to *implement* fully the budget requirements. Latin *implere* (to fill up).

transitory — C: Temporary; existing for a short time only; as, a political alliance that is more than *transitory*. Latin *transire* (to pass).

flag — B: Lose strength or weaken; as, their efforts *flagged*. Perhaps from Old Norse *flakka* (to flutter).

interdiction — A: Decree that forbids or prohibits; as, *interdictions* against free speech. Latin *interdicere* (to stop, outlaw).

format — D: General structure or arrangement; as, The meeting will have an inflexible *format*. Latin *formare* (to shape).

extraneous — D: Irrelevant; not related to or pertinent; as, *extraneous* developments. Latin *extraneus* (external, foreign).

sequester — C: Withdraw; set apart; seize; as, to *sequester* or withhold funds to meet government deficit targets. Also, to seclude; as, the jury was *sequestered* in a hotel. Latin *sequestrare* (to surrender for safekeeping).

mediator — B: Person who tries to bring about an agreement in disputes; as, *Mediators* helped resolve the boundary conflict. Latin *mediare* (to be in the middle).

resolute — A: Showing great determination; steady in purpose; unwavering; as, a *resolute* commitment to saving the environment. Latin *resolvere* (to resolve).

Vocabulary Ratings
9 — 11 correct . . . Good
12 — 17 correct . . . Excellent
18 — 20 correct . . . Exceptional

66When you get to be President, there are the honours, the 21-gun salutes, all those things. You have to remember it isn't for you. It's for the Presidency.**99**

—Harry S. Truman quoted by Merle Miller in Plain Speaking (Putnam)

CRIME AND PUNISHMENT

Never out of the news, crime also features prominently in fiction and drama. In this identification parade of terms from the language of crime and punishment, select the answer you think is nearest in meaning to the key word. Turn the page to check your score.

apprehend — A: permit. B: improve. C: seize. D: condemn.

bogus — A: threatening. B: fake. C: boastful. D: remote.

manslaughter — A: massacre. B: attempted murder. C: retribution. D: unplanned killing.

collude — A: conspire. B: disagree. C: persist. D: hide.

forensic — relating to A: international police work. B: courts of law. C: victim support. D: crime prevention.

incarcerate — A: instruct. B: disable. C: imprison. D: provoke.

summary — A: harsh. B: eminent. C: comfortable. D: brief.

corroborate — A: recollect. B: confirm. C: intimidate. D: postpone.

recidivist — A: a dealer in stolen goods. B: prison visitor. C: persistent criminal. D: informer.

allege — A: assert. B: co-operate. C: link. D: simulate.

homicidal — A: fanatical. B: in despair. C: sympathetic. D: murderous.

remand — A: blame. B: send back. C: withdraw. D: express regret.

66In any contest between power and patience, bet on patience.**99**

—W. B. PRESCOTT

circumstantial — A: fabricated. B: trivial. C: indirect.
     D: long-winded.
duress — A: pressure. B: insolence. C: cruelty.
     D: isolation.
nefarious — A: uncommon. B: absent-minded. C: agitated.
     D: wicked.
purloin — A: corrupt. B: discover. C: steal. D: infiltrate.
deposition — A: statement. B: hardship. C: departure.
     D: payment.
indict — A: point out. B: charge. C: tolerate. D: protest.
delinquent — A: fragile. B: hysterical. C: inexperienced.
     D: offending.
contraband — A: deceitful plan. B: warning. C: denial.
     D: smuggled goods.

ANSWERS

apprehend — C: Seize; arrest. "Police *apprehended* the accused at the scene of the crime." Latin *ad-* (to) and *prehendere* (lay hold of).

bogus — B: Fake; not genuine. "A *bogus* official tried to gain entry to the pensioner's home." American, of unknown origin.

manslaughter — D: Unplanned killing; in law, unlawful killing without malice aforethought. "Following the fatal accident, the driver was charged with *manslaughter.*" Old English *mann* and Old Norse *slatr* (butchered meat).

collude — A: Conspire; act together secretly. "The two suspects had *colluded* over their statements to the police." Latin *com-* (together) and *ludere* (to play).

forensic — B: Relating to courts of law; as, *forensic* evidence. Latin *forensis* (public), from forum, the principal meeting-place in ancient Roman cities.

incarcerate — C: Imprison. "Judges have the power to *incarcerate* convicted offenders." Latin *in-* (in) and *carcer* (prison).

summary — D: Brief; without formalities; as, the *summary* justice meted out by the lynch mob. Latin *summa* (sum).

corroborate — B: Confirm; provide supporting evidence. "His story was *corroborated* by witnesses." Latin *com-* and *roborare* (to strengthen).

recidivist — C: Persistent criminal; one who relapses into crime; as, a hopeless *recidivist* who had served several prison sentences. Latin *re-* (back) and *cadere* (to fall).

allege — A: Assert; make an accusation without proof; as, the *alleged* assault. Latin *allegare* (to despatch).

homicidal — D: Murderous; likely to kill; as, a *homicidal* maniac. Latin *homo* (man) and *caedere* (to kill).

remand — B: Send back. "Judges *remanded* the prisoner in custody for seven days." Latin *re-* and *mandare* (to command).

circumstantial — C: Indirect; concerning matters surrounding an event rather than the event itself; as, guilt inferred from *circumstantial* evidence. Latin *circum* (around) and *stare* (to stand).

duress — A: Pressure; coercion; as, a confession obtained under *duress.* Latin *durus* (hard).

nefarious — D: Wicked. "The arrest brought an end to the terrorist's *nefarious* career." Latin *ne-* (not) and *fas* (divine law).

purloin — C: Steal. "He was caught in possession of a *purloined* cheque." Old French *purloigner* (to put away).

deposition — A: A statement or evidence given under oath. "The court heard the victim's evidence in a *deposition* made from her hospital bed." Latin *de-* (from) and *ponere* (to place).

indict — B: Charge with a crime. "He was *indicted* on six counts of burglary." Latin *in-* (towards) and *dicere* (to say).

delinquent — D: Offending, usually in a minor way. "The youth had a history of *delinquent* behaviour." Latin *de-* and *linquere* (to leave).

contraband — D: Smuggled goods. "Customs officers seized *contraband* at the border." Italian *contra* (against) and *bando* (proclamation).

Vocabulary Ratings
> 9 — 11 correct . . . Good
> 12 — 17 correct . . . Excellent
> 18 — 20 correct . . . Exceptional

OUT ON A LIMERICK

There once was a man of verbosity
Who loved words with savage ferocity;
Waxing profound,
He fell to the ground,
Knocked out by his own pomposity

—M. Venita Victoria

THE GOSPELS

Much of the glorious language in the King James Bible, first published in 1611, is still in use today. How well do you know the following words from the Gospels? Select the word or phrase nearest in meaning to the key word. Turn the page for your score.

parable — A: handicap. B: story. C: winding road. D: hoe.

perdition — A: awareness. B: danger. C: damnation. D: wilderness.

consultation — A: meeting. B: insulting gesture. C: infection. D: treaty.

abundance — A: desertion. B: great activity. C: group. D: large amount.

lamentation — A: flesh wound. B: sorrow. C: greed. D: birdsong.

iniquity — A: hostility. B: speed. C: imbalance. D: wickedness.

pinnacle — A: a game. B: turret. C: fastening. D: boat.

resurrection — A: tall building. B: revival. C: rebellion. D: tension.

err — A: correct. B: originate. C: be wrong. D: pretend.

whit — A: trick. B: particle. C: wood-shaving. D: funny man.

trespass — A: offend. B: support. C: win over. D: defraud.

expedient — A: courageous. B: simple. C: anticipated. D: advantageous.

repentance — A: imprisonment. B: regret. C: sloping roof. D: debt.

❝Humour is laughing at what you haven't got when you ought to have it.**❞**

—LANGSTON HUGHES

---

merciful — A: compassionate. B: thankful. C: joyous.
     D: foolish.
premeditate — A: be early. B: choose carefully. C: plan ahead.
     D: offer counselling.
perplexed — A: twofold. B: bewildered. C: distressed.
     D: see-through.
endure — A: make dear. B: try. C: last. D: compel.
tempest — A: storm. B: attractive woman. C: fortified temple.
     D: allowance.
indignation — A: poverty. B: disapproval. C: impairment.
     D: anger.
testimony — A: precious metal. B: will. C: stolen coins.
     D: declaration.

---

parable — B: Story told to illustrate a moral or spiritual lesson. "And he began to speak unto them by *parables.*" Latin *parabola* (comparison).

perdition — C: Damnation, eternal death; as, "None of them is lost, but the son of *perdition.*" Latin *perdere* (to destroy).

consultation — A: Meeting to seek advice or information; a conference; as, "The chief priests held a *consultation* with the elders and scribes." Latin *consultatio.*

adundance — D: Large amount. "For all these have of their *abundance* cast in unto the offerings of God." Latin *abundantia.*

lamentation — B: Sorrow, the expressing of grief. "In Rama was there a voice heard, *lamentation,* and weeping, and great mourning." Old French.

iniquity — D: Wickedness; gross injustice. "And because *iniquity* shall abound, the love of many shall wax cold." Latin *iniquitas.*

pinnacle — B: Turret; as, "a *pinnacle* of the temple." Latin *pinna* (wing).

resurrection — B: Revival; rising from the dead. "Jesus said unto her, I am the *resurrection,* and the life." Late Latin *resurrectio.*

err — C: Be or do wrong. "Ye do *err,* not knowing the scriptures, nor the power of God." Latin *errare* (to stray).

whit — B: A particle, the least amount; as, "clean every *whit.*" Fifteenth-century English.

trespass — A: Offend. "If thy brother *trespass* against thee, rebuke him." Also to infringe upon. Old French *trespasser* (to pass over).

expedient — D: Advantageous; also appropriate. "It is *expedient* for you that I go away." Latin *expedire* (to put in order).

repentance — B: Regret for one's actions; resolution to cease wrongdoing; as, "I am not come to call the righteous, but sinners to *repentance.*" Latin *paenitere* (to repent).

merciful — A: Compassionate, showing forbearance towards some-one. "Be ye therefore *merciful,* as your Father also is *merci-ful.*" Latin *merces* (reward).

premeditate — C: Plan ahead; as, "Take no thought beforehand what ye shall speak, neither do ye *premeditate.*" Latin *prae* (before) and *meditari* (to contemplate).

perplexed — B: Bewildered, disconcerted; as, "He was *perplexed,* because that it was said of some, that John was risen from the dead." Latin *plectere* (to plait).

endure — C: Last, remain in existence. "But he that shall *endure* unto the end, the same shall be saved." Also to undergo. Latin *indurare* (to harden).

tempest — A: Storm, particularly a violently windy one. "And, behold, there arose a great *tempest* in the sea." Old French.

indignation — D: Anger at a supposed injustice. "And the ruler of the synagogue answered with *indignation.*" Latin *indignatio.*

testimony — D: Declaration; evidence; as, "We know that his *testi-mony* is true." Latin *testimonium.*

Vocabulary Ratings

> 9 — 11 correct . . . Good
> 12 — 17 correct . . . Excellent
> 18 — 20 correct . . . Exceptional

❝One filled with joy preaches without preaching.❞

—MOTHER TERESA

SPEAKING OUT

Radio phone-in shows provide many people the chance to speak out and be heard. The following words may help you sound off more clearly and forcefully if you decide to phone in yourself. Mark the answers you think are correct, then turn the page to check your score.

sumptuous — A: silky. B: lavish. C: light and airy.
D: austere.

cascade — A: cliff. B: mountain ridge. C: waterfall.
D: butte.

insatiable — A: impossible to satisfy. B: having strong feelings.
C: requiring continual effort. D: immovable.

fetish — A: sudden notion. B: erratic behaviour.
C: feeling of obligation. D: object of obsessive devotion.

penchant — A: plan. B: liking for something.
C: decorative banner. D: dreamy thoughtfulness.

explicit — A: inflexible. B: knowledgeable. C: clear.
D: intricate.

arcana — A: remembrances. B: main points. C: mysteries.
D: difficulties.

frippery — A: wit. B: solemnity. C: trickery. D: showiness.

redress — A: express disapproval. B: evoke. C: consume.
D: rectify.

alleviate — A: assemble. B: interfere. C: lessen. D: claim.

❝How much easier it is to be critical than to be
correct.**❞**

—BENJAMIN DISRAELI

There is always hope when people are forced to listen to both sides.

—JOHN STUART MILL

---

scurrilous — A: abusive. B: scrubbed and clean. C: lacking swiftness. D: shocking.

mendacious — A: tattered. B: outrageous. C: not truthful. D: poor.

vindication — A: slander. B: justification. C: attack. D: self-righteous pose.

commemorate — A: flatter. B: enjoy. C: memorise. D: honour.

meld — A: soothe. B: merge. C: purchase. D: glisten.

mordant — A: deadly. B: alarming. C: sombre. D: sharply sarcastic.

proselytise — A: confront. B: establish. C: be made known. D: try to convert.

duplicity — A: repetition. B: probity. C: deceit. D: imitation.

hegemony — A: unlawfulness. B: dominance. C: mass migration. D: democracy.

rant — A: speak wildly. B: praise inordinately. C: formalise. D: treat with scorn.

sumptuous — B: Lavish; costly and luxurious; magnificent; as, a *sumptuous* celebration. Latin *sumptus* (expense).

cascade — C: Waterfall descending over a steep and rocky surface. Also, anything that resembles a waterfall; as, a *cascade* of flowers covering the railing. Italian *cascata*.

insatiable — A: Impossible to satisfy; never getting enough; greedy; as, the leader's *insatiable* drive for power. Latin *insatiabilis*.

fetish — D: An object or activity receiving obsessive or irrational devotion; as, to make a *fetish* of sports. Latin *facticius* (artificial).

penchant — B: Strong liking or inclination for something; as, a *penchant* for politics. Old French *pencher* (to incline).

explicit — C: Clear and precise, leaving no doubt as to meaning; as, The general gave an *explicit* explanation. Latin *ex-* (out) and *plicare* (to fold).

arcana — C: Mysteries; information known only to those involved; as, an attempt to expose a secret society's *arcana*. Latin *arcere* (to shut in).

frippery — D: Pretentious showiness in dress or manners; as, disdain for *frippery* of any kind. Old French *freperie* (old clothes).

redress — D: To remedy or rectify a wrongdoing; as, charity and volunteerism are simple ways to *redress* social problems. Middle French *redresser*.

alleviate — C: Lessen or make less severe; as, the medicine helps *alleviate* her pain. Latin *ad-* and *levis* (light).

scurrilous — A: Abusive and insulting; coarse; vulgar; as, The talk-show host grew tired of the *scurrilous* attacks on him. Latin *scurrilis* (jeering).

mendacious — C: Not truthful; lying or false; as, Voters complained about the *mendacious* statements of party old-timers. Latin *mendax*.

vindication — B: Justification; clearance of blame or guilt; as, the *vindication* of a controversial policy when it turns out to be successful. Latin *vindicare* (to claim).

commemorate — D: Honour or celebrate someone or something; as, The monument *commemorates* those who fell in battle. Latin *commemorare*.

meld — B: Merge, blend or unite; as, His graceful letters *melded* many different people into a political party. Blend of *melt* and *weld*.

mordant — D: Sharply or bitingly sarcastic or cutting; as, the cartoonist's *mordant* observations. Latin *mordere* (to bite).

proselytise — D: Try to convert a person from one belief or faith to another. Greek *proserchesthai* (to approach).

duplicity — C: Deceit; deliberate deceptiveness; as, a broker's *duplicity* in selling phony stocks. Latin *duplex* (twofold).

hegemony — B: Dominance of one state or thing over another; as, Talk shows weaken the *hegemony* of more conventional organs of opinion. Greek *hegemonia* (leadership).

rant — A: Speak wildly or in a loud, extravagant way; as, The agitator *ranted* for hours. Old Dutch *ranten* (to talk foolishly).

Vocabulary Ratings

    9 — 11 correct ... Good
    12 — 17 correct ... Excellent
    18 — 20 correct ... Exceptional

Obnoxious guest replying to hostess's comment: "Me?

Argumentative and pretentious? Au contraire!"

—HOEST, KING FEATURES

FROM JANE AUSTEN'S PEN

Immaculately observed, witty yet profound, the novels of Jane Austen, who died 180 years ago, continue to delight. In this list of words from her books, select the word or phrase you believe is nearest in meaning to the key word. Turn the page for your score.

eligible — A: readable. B: permitted by law. C: suitable. D: easy to understand.

cavil — A: object. B: hesitate. C: warn. D: deceive.

solace — A: loneliness. B: consolation. C: thrift. D: patience.

dilatory — A: industrious. B: swollen. C: defiant. D: slow.

impropriety — A: accusation. B: incorrectness. C: desire. D: presumption.

circumspection — A: curiosity. B: avoidance. C: description. D: caution.

obviate — A: explain. B: dispose of. C: yield. D: contradict.

heinous — A: proud. B: impulsive. C: distracted. D: atrocious.

conjecture — A: praise. B: guess. C: appeal. D: disregard.

inured — A: accustomed. B: well-informed. C: innocent. D: opinionated.

rectitude — A: shyness. B: disregard of danger. C: cruelty. D: moral uprightness.

comply — A: take advice. B: make a collection. C: act in accordance. D: protest.

66Liberty is the only thing you cannot have unless you are willing to give it to others.**99**

—WILLIAM ALLEN WHITE

66There are two types of people—those who come into a room and say, 'Well, here I am!' and those who come in and say, 'Ah, there you are.'99

—FREDERIC COLLINS

---

deference — A: respect. B: doubt. C: obstinacy. D: enthusiasm.

supplant — A: add to. B: restrict. C: take the place of. D: hold up.

hackneyed — A: sensitive to criticism. B: humourless. C: out of touch. D: overused.

retract — A: repay. B: withdraw. C: answer back. D: delay.

fickleness — A: weakness. B: incompetence. C: aggression. D: changeability.

engross — A: dedicate. B: give approval. C: preoccupy. D: make commitment.

unequivocal — A: varying quality. B: overwhelming. C: unmistakable. D: faultless.

dissipation — A: squandering. B: evangelism. C: separation. D: discord.

66One of the most dangerous forms of human error is forgetting what one is trying to achieve.99

—PAUL NITZE

 *ANSWERS*

eligible — C: Suitable; entitled to be chosen. "Mr. Collins's present circumstances made it a most *eligible* match for their daughter." Latin *e-* (out) and *legere* (to pick).

cavil — A: Object on false or trivial grounds; as, "Anne, far from wishing to *cavil* at the pleasure." Latin *cavillari* (to mock).

solace — B: Consolation; comfort. "The business of her life was to get her daughters married: its *solace* was visiting and news." Latin *solari* (to console).

dilatory — D: Slow; given to delaying. "Though *dilatory* in undertaking business, he was quick in its execution." Latin *dilatorious* (delaying).

impropriety — B: Incorrectness of behaviour. "She was now struck with the *impropriety* of such communications to a stranger." Latin *improprius* (not proper).

circumspection — D: Caution; taking everything into account. "The lessons of her past folly might teach her humility and *circumspection* in the future." Latin *circum* (round) and *specere* (to look).

obviate — B: To dispose of; get round. "That will *obviate* all difficulties." Latin *ob-* (against) and *via* (way).

heinous — D: Atrocious; extremely wicked. "Leave her to reap the fruits of her own *heinous* offence." Old French *haïneus* (hateful).

conjecture — B: Guess. "As to his future situation, he could *conjecture* very little about it." Latin *con-* (together) and *jacere* (to throw).

inured — A: Accustomed; hardened. "A younger son, you know, must be *inured* to self-denial and independence." Old French *en-* (in) and *eure* (work).

rectitude — D: Moral uprightness; as, "Her sister, of whose *rectitude* and delicacy she was sure her opinion could never be shaken." Latin *rectus* (right).

comply — C: Act in accordance. "You will hardly blame her for refusing to *comply* with this entreaty." Latin *complere* (to fill up).

deference — A: Respect; courtesy to a superior. "She is the sort of woman whom one cannot regard with too much *deference*." Latin *de-* (down) and *ferre* (to bring).

supplant — C: Take the place of. "Robert Martin had thoroughly *supplanted* Mr. Knightley." Latin *sub* (under) and *planta* (sole).

hackneyed — D: Overused; made commonplace through repetition. "That expression of violently in love is so *hackneyed*." Middle English, perhaps from *Hackney* in London, where hire-horses ("hacks") were pastured.

retract — B: Withdraw; cancel. "I hope you do not *retract* what you then said." Latin *re-* (back) and *trahere* (to draw).

fickleness — D: Changeability. "Songs and proverbs, all talk of woman's *fickleness*." Old English *ficol,* also *gefic* (deceit).

engross — C: Preoccupy; monopolise attention. "His business *engrosses* him." French *en gros* (wholesale).

unequivocal — C: Unmistakable; not ambiguous. "Your meaning must be *unequivocal*." Latin *in-* (not), *aequus* (equal) and *vocare* (to call).

dissipation — A: Squandering; wasteful or intemperate living. "His life was a life of idleness and *dissipation*." Latin *dissipare* (to throw away).

Vocabulary Ratings

9 — 11 correct . . . Good

12 — 17 correct . . . Excellent

18 — 20 correct . . . Exceptional

FROM HAND TO HAND

You and I are connected, one way or another, with everyone else who occupies Planet Earth. Test your knowledge of inter-relationships among people,

places and things. How many of the following words do you know? Turn the page to find your score.

resource — A: protection. B: urgent claim. C: beginning or origin. D: available supply.

matriarch — woman who A: has many children. B: rules a family. C: is of noble birth. D: is energetic.

amity — A: wealth. B: mirth. C: good will. D: a sharing.

catholic — A: local. B: energetic. C: devout. D: universal.

familial — relating to A: fame. B: comfort. C: food shortages. D: family.

surname — A: two or more names. B: first name. C: new name. D: family name.

amenable — A: capable. B: hopeful. C: cheerful. D: agreeable.

kindred — A: variegated. B: related. C: inattentive. D: sensitive.

unilateral — A: one-sided. B: alike. C: invalid. D: unanimous.

synergy — A: state of equilibrium. B: effect of wrongdoing. C: individual effort. D: combined action of separate components.

altruism — A: introspection. B: hypocrisy. C: unselfishness. D: idealization.

66He who helps early helps twice.**99**

—TADEUSZ MAZOWIECKI, PRIME MINISTER OF POLAND

> **"** Do not commit the error, common among the young, of assuming that if you cannot save the whole of mankind you have failed. **"**
>
> —Jan de Hartog, The Lamb's War (Harper & Row)

---

reconciliation — A: re-establishment of friendship.
B: diplomatic manoeuvring. C: conversion.
D: tactfulness.

spouse — A: principal heir. B: newlywed. C: guardian.
D: husband or wife.

magnanimity — A: hearty enjoyment. B: great enthusiasm.
C: nobility of spirit. D: soundness of judgement.

nexus — A: something that naturally follows. B: connection.
C: veto. D: secret intrigue.

consanguineous — A: having the same ancestor. B: insular.
C: peaceful. D: fair and just.

fidelity — A: health. B: playfulness. C: loyalty. D: remoteness.

collegial — relating to A: genealogy. B: an assembly of diverse
pieces. C: friendliness. D: a group of colleagues.

comity — A: beauty. B: courtesy. C: wisdom. D: suspicion.

compassion — A: congeniality. B: spirituality. C: sympathy.
D: intolerance.

 *ANSWERS*

resource — D: Available supply that can be used as needed; as, to conserve *resources* for future generations. Latin *resurgere* (to rise again).

matriarch — B: Woman who rules or leads her family, tribe or organisation. Latin *matri-* (mother) and Greek *archos* (ruler).

amity — C: Good will; friendship; peaceful relationship, especially between nations. Latin *amicus* (friend).

catholic — D: Universal; concerning or including all; as, having *catholic* tastes in literature. Greek *katholikos*.

familial — D: Relating to or characteristic of a family; as, a *familial* trait of becoming entrepreneurs. Latin *familia* (household).

surname — D: Family or last name, as opposed to a first name. French *sur* (over, above) and English *name*.

amenable — D: Agreeable; having an open mind and being willing to listen; as, Both sides were *amenable* to a settlement of the border dispute. Old French *amener* (to lead).

kindred — B: Pertaining to a person's relatives. Also, having a similar nature; as, *kindred* feelings. Middle English *kinreden*.

unilateral — A: One-sided; done by only one or a few people, groups or nations; as, *Unilateral* action may be positive or harmful, depending on circumstances. Latin *unilateralis*.

synergy — D: Combined action of separate components, making the total effect greater than the sum of the individual effects; as, the creative *synergy* of Gilbert and Sullivan musicals. Greek *synergia* (co-operation).

altruism — C: Unselfish concern for the welfare of others; as, the *altruism* of nations that send food to starving people in other lands. Italian *altrui* (of others).

reconciliation — A: Re-establishment of a friendship or relationship; settlement of a dispute. Latin *re-* (again) and *conciliare* (to bring together).

spouse — D: Husband or wife. Latin *sponsus* (betrothed).

magnanimity — C: Nobility of spirit; generosity in overlooking insults or injuries; as, the *magnanimity* of Abraham Lincoln. Latin *magnus* (great) and *animus* (spirit).

nexus — B: Connection, link, bond between individuals of a group or parts of a series; as, the *nexus* between doe and fawn. Latin *nectere* (to bind).

consanguineous — A: Having the same ancestor; related by blood; as, The recent immigrants realised they were *consanguineous*. Latin *con-* (with) and *sanguineus* (of blood).

fidelity — C: Loyalty; as, her *fidelity* to the ideals of democracy. Also, exactness. Latin *fidelis* (faithful).

collegial — D: Relating to a group of colleagues, each of whom has equal authority; as, *Collegial* deliberations can be lengthy, inconclusive and frustrating. Latin *collega* (associate, fellow).

comity — B: Courtesy, especially between nations in recognising laws and customs; as, the importance of international *comity*. Latin *comis* (polite, kind).

compassion — C: Sympathy. Latin *com-* (together) and *pati* (to suffer). Therefore, a person acting with *compassion* literally shares in the suffering of another; as, *compassionate* emergency rescue-squad volunteers.

Vocabulary Ratings
   9 — 11 correct . . . Good
   12 — 17 correct . . . Excellent
   18 — 20 correct . . . Exceptional

66We ought to think that we are one of the leaves of a tree, and the tree is all humanity. We cannot live without the others, without the tree.**99**

—PABLO CASALS

*The appealing or comforting words that follow, if appropriately
spoken, may help to improve relationships and negotiations or
enhance the quality of life. Turn the page to see how many of your
answers are correct.*

compatible — A: desirable. B: gentle. C: harmonious.
   D: likable.

conciliatory — A: patient. B: wise. C: careful.
   D: accommodating.

facilitate — A: pretend. B: congratulate. C: create.
   D: make easier.

auspicious — A: unlikely. B: trusting. C: free from suspicion.
   D: favourable.

veracity — A: truthfulness. B: eagerness. C: perseverance.
   D: outspokenness.

accolade — A: praise. B: prudent advice. C: celebration.
   D: soothing words.

commiserate — A: forgive. B: pity. C: tolerate. D: be grateful.

magnanimous — A: bighearted. B: wondrous. C: optimistic.
   D: unprejudiced.

cordiality — A: sincere graciousness. B: toast to friendship.
   C: deep concern. D: responsiveness.

perspicacious — A: lucid. B: insightful. C: talkative.
   D: painstaking.

66Words of comfort, skilfully administered,

are the oldest therapy known to man.**99**

—LOUIS NIZER

> **66** The Bible tells us to love our neighbours, and also to love our enemies; probably because they are generally the same people. **99**
>
> —G. K. CHESTERTON

radiant — A: spellbinding. B: welcoming. C: humorous.
    D: bright and happy.

cosset — A: whisper. B: sing softly. C: pamper. D: play games.

incisive — A: uncertain. B: hardheaded. C: bitter.
    D: penetrating.

largess — A: thoughtfulness. B: gift. C: good report.
    D: great imagination.

beguile — A: persuade. B: cause to smile. C: charm.
    D: make free from guilt.

meritorious — A: well-known. B: extremely learned.
    C: deserving praise. D: brave.

ameliorate — A: improve. B: appease. C: approve.
    D: ingratiate.

incentive — A: creative thought. B: stimulus. C: excitement.
    D: ambition.

humane — A: sentimental. B: kind. C: self-effacing.
    D: well-meaning.

tranquil — A: modest. B: airy. C: effortless. D: calm.

> **66** The right word may be effective, but no word was ever as effective as a rightly timed pause. **99**
>
> —MARK TWAIN

compatible — C: Harmonious; working together well; congenial; as, *compatible* partners; *compatible* software. Latin *com-* (with) and *pati* (to suffer).

conciliatory — D: Accommodating; trying to overcome hostility; as, The U.N. Security Council members made *conciliatory* efforts. Latin *conciliare* (to bring together).

facilitate — D: Make easier; help remove impediments; as, to *facilitate* immigration procedures. Latin *facere* (to do).

auspicious — D: Favourable; predicting success; as, an *auspicious* beginning of a negotiation. Latin *auspicium* (prediction based on observing bird flight).

veracity — A: Truthfulness; accuracy; as, The accountant's *veracity* is unquestioned. Latin *veracitas*.

accolade — A: Praise; award; honour; acclaim; as, The teacher deserved the school's *accolade*. Also, a touch with a sword conferring knighthood. French *accoler* (to embrace).

commiserate — B: Pity or express sympathy for another's pain or distress; as, to *commiserate* with earthquake victims. Latin *com-* (with) and *miserari* (to pity).

magnanimous — A: Bighearted; noble; forgiving. Latin *magnus* (great) and *animus* (mind, soul).

cordiality — A: Sincere graciousness and friendliness; as, The elderly gentleman welcomed us with *cordiality*. Latin *cordialis* (of the heart).

perspicacious — B: Having penetrating insight to understand what is hidden or puzzling; shrewd; as, a *perspicacious* judge of character. Latin *perspicere* (to see through).

radiant — D: Bright and happy; expressing joy, love and well-being; as, her *radiant* expression. Latin *radiare* (to radiate).

cosset — C: Pamper; coddle; give special attention to; as, to *cosset* the one you love. Origin uncertain.

incisive — D: Penetrating; sharp; keen; clear and direct; as, an *incisive* explanation. Latin *incidere* (to cut into).

largess — **B:** A generous gift of favours or money; as, the *largess* given by a foundation for an important cause. French *large* (generous).

beguile — **C:** Charm, enchant, delight; as, Dr. Seuss's stories *beguile* old and young alike. Also, to deceive slyly. Middle English *bigilen* (to deceive).

meritorious — **C:** Deserving praise, honour or reward; as, public acclaim for *meritorious* service to his country. Latin *meritorius* (earning money).

ameliorate — **A:** Improve, or at least make tolerable, unfortunate situations, suggesting partial relief; as, to *ameliorate* the problems of the homeless. Latin *melior* (better).

incentive — **B:** Stimulus; motivating influence; as, a financial *incentive* to eliminate pollution. Latin *incinere* (to sing).

humane — **B:** Kind; compassionate; considerate; as, a *humane* nurse. Latin *humanus* (human).

tranquil — **D:** Calm; quiet; peaceful; as, the *tranquil* presence of the chaplain. Latin *tranquillus*.

Vocabulary Ratings
> 9 — 11 correct . . . Good
> 12 — 17 correct . . . Excellent
> 18 — 20 correct . . . Exceptional

❝Sainthood emerges when you can listen to someone's tale of woe and not respond with a description of your own.**❞**
—ANDREW V. MASON, M.D.

NOT TO BE CONFUSED WITH . . .

People sometimes misunderstand each other because of confusion over a key word or a phrase spoken carelessly or in haste. How many of the following words are you absolutely sure you know? Turn the page to check your score.

lingo — A: pidgin English. B: enunciation. C: type of dance. D: jargon.

incredulous — A: astounding. B: amusing. C: contradictory. D: sceptical.

expound — A: release. B: be pompous. C: explain. D: belittle.

magisterial — A: manipulative. B: controversial. C: cautious. D: authoritative.

abomination — A: something hateful. B: extreme difficulty. C: curse. D: sense of helplessness.

strident — A: hysterical. B: offensively loud. C: ambitious. D: strict and severe.

delve — A: muddle. B: put away. C: investigate. D: swoop.

integral — A: essential. B: truthful. C: temporary. D: logical.

gaggle — A: surprised stare. B: choking laughter. C: cluster. D: restraint.

ineptitude — A: unfitness. B: elimination. C: carelessness. D: remoteness.

❝People generally quarrel because they cannot argue.**❞**

—G. K. CHESTERTON

---

dishevelled — A: unmanageable. B: deeply upset. C: untidy.
D: scantily clothed.

factor — A: suggest. B: produce. C: calculate. D: change.

broker — A: confront. B: negotiate. C: deceive. D: dismiss.

latitude — A: firmness. B: listlessness. C: lively interest.
D: room to move.

assiduously — A: diligently. B: bitterly. C: mockingly. D: excitedly.

snippet — A: sassy remark. B: small jewelled clasp. C: fragment.
D: complaint.

civility — A: legal procedure. B: politeness. C: peacefulness.
D: loyalty.

conceit — A: traditional ceremony. B: bold lie. C: generosity.
D: fanciful idea.

assuage — A: convert. B: guarantee. C: relieve. D: startle.

brawny — A: muscular. B: argumentative. C: pushy.
D: menacing.

GOOD QUESTION!

Is there a difference between a fat chance and a slim chance?

—Robert T. Schwartz

Why can't we just spell it *orderves*?

—Holly Thompson

lingo — D: Jargon or slang of a particular group or field of study, often unfamiliar to others; as, the *lingo* of astronomers. Latin *lingua* (tongue).

incredulous — D: Sceptical; expressing doubt; as, trying to persuade *incredulous* potential customers. Latin *in-* (not) and *credere* (to believe).

expound — C: Explain in detail; clarify; as, The gardener *expounded* at length on the benefits of bees in the garden. Latin *exponere* (to put forth).

magisterial — D: Authoritative; as, a *magisterial* study of World War I. Also, domineering, pompous. Latin *magister* (master).

abomination — A: Something hateful or detestable; as, the *abomination* of genocide. Latin *abominari* (to hate, detest).

strident — B: Offensively loud and insistent; harsh and grating; as, The *strident* coach generated excitement, anger and a brawling brand of football. Latin *stridere* (to make a harsh sound).

delve — C: Investigate carefully; research intensively; as, to *delve* into a mysterious cave. Old English *delfan* (to dig).

integral — A: Essential for completeness; as, The programme is an *integral* part of his economic plan. Latin *integer* (whole).

gaggle — C: Cluster or group, often disorderly; as, a *gaggle* of questionable gambling companions. Also, a flock of geese. Middle English *gagelen* (to cackle).

ineptitude — A: Unfitness; foolishness; lack of good judgement; as, Arrogance and *ineptitude* led to the team's miserable record last season. Latin *ineptus* (not suitable).

dishevelled — C: Untidy in personal appearance; unkempt; as, the bleary-eyed, *dishevelled* composer. Old French *descheveler* (to disarrange the hair).

factor — C: Calculate or include as a necessary element in planning; as, The car manufacturer tries to *factor* in safety, comfort and performance. Latin *facere* (to make or do).

broker — B: Negotiate or arrange in order to influence an outcome; as, He tried to *broker* a new approach to flood-insurance legislation. Old Norman French *broceor*.

latitude — D: Room to move; freedom from restrictions; as, Colleges allow students almost unlimited *latitude* in their personal lives. Also, distance north or south of the equator. Latin *latus* (wide).

assiduously — A: Diligently; persistently; as, He pressed *assiduously* for a simplification of tax instructions. Latin *assidere* (to sit at).

snippet — C: Fragment; scrap; small bit or portion; as, a *snippet* of information. English *snip*.

civility — B: Politeness; courteous behaviour; as, the lack of *civility* on many TV talk shows. Latin *civilis* (civil).

conceit — D: Fanciful or clever idea or expression; as, In a nice little *conceit*, the writer was visited by her fictional character. Also, exaggerated self-opinion. Middle English *conceiven* (to conceive).

assuage — C: Relieve or lessen pain or want; as, His kind words *assuaged* the family's grief. Latin *ad* (to) and *suavis* (sweet).

brawny — A: Muscular and strong; as, He was the smallest of a *brawny* family. Old English *braedan*.

Vocabulary Ratings

        9 — 11 correct . . . Good

        12 — 17 correct . . . Excellent

        18 — 20 correct . . . Exceptional

❝All you need in this life is ignorance and confidence, and then success is sure.**❞**

—*MARK TWAIN*

GETTING TO THE POINT

Short words are like firecrackers with a short fuse: they get to the point quickly. Often they are packed with as much information as their longer-fused relatives. All the words in this test have only one syllable. But watch out—short doesn't mean easy. Turn the page for your results.

taut — A: tough. B: tight. C: skimpy and revealing. D: believable.

churn — A: stir violently. B: back and fill. C: twist and turn. D: go in circles.

mesh — A: throw together carelessly. B: separate out. C: co-ordinate. D: involve.

boot — (with computers) A: shut down. B: eliminate software. C: change programs. D: start up.

squib — A: young bird. B: small sea animal. C: sudden gush. D: short news item.

brood — A: worry about. B: treasure or cherish. C: cover or spread. D: exact revenge.

grist — A: dust. B: grief. C: essence. D: grain.

thrum — A: play a stringed instrument. B: scan. C: rock back and forth. D: smooth over.

rasp — A: silk cloth. B: cold blast. C: feather. D: harsh sound.

POINTS OF VIEW

I'm trusting. You're naive. He's a fool. —Lori A. Abrams

I'm quiet. You're unassertive. He's a wimp. —Alexandra Frank

I'm sensitive. You're fussy. He's neurotic. —Michele Simos

I'm concerned. You're curious. He's nosy. —Lori A. Abrams

I'm thrifty. You're a bit tight. He's cheap. —Rosemary Proehl

Summarising a book: "Once you put it down, you can't pick it up."

—BERNARD BRADEN, BBC

bleak — A: harassed. B: plain and simple. C: dreary.
   D: quiet and demure.
wane — A: grow. B: decrease. C: minimize. D: vanish.
quail — A: ease. B: lose courage. C: be humble. D: hide.
zeal — A: delight. B: frenzy. C: fervour. D: stamina.
bane — A: act of prohibiting. B: significant document.
   C: area or domain. D: cause of misery.
gig — A: joke. B: mistake. C: lie. D: job.
rime — A: frost. B: edge. C: salt. D: groove.
fend — A: rebuild. B: repel. C: restrain. D: attack.
preen — A: elaborate. B: masquerade as. C: dress up.
   D: lament.
cairn — A: ornate vase. B: ghostly presence. C: castle tower.
   D: mound of stones.
fell — A: fierce. B: extensive. C: slippery. D: heavy.

HOW COLD IS IT?

Cold as a cast-iron commode on the shady side of an iceberg

Cold as a polar bear's pajamas —Larry Wright

Cold! If the thermometer were an inch longer we'd all freeze to death! —Mark Twain

 *ANSWERS*

taut — B: Tight; as, The inexperienced young rider held the reins very *taut*. Also tense; as *taut* nerves. Middle English *toght*.

churn — A: Stir or agitate violently; as, The raging storm *churned* the sea. Old English *cyrne*.

mesh — C: Co-ordinate; combine; as, The couple made an effort to *mesh* their careers. Also, to interlock, as with gears. Old English *max* (a net).

boot — D: Start up a computer, loading its memory with the information it needs to function. Derived from *bootstrap*.

squib — D: Short news item, often used as filler material in a publication. Also, a small firework. Origin unknown.

brood — A: Worry about; focus on a subject obsessively and silently; as, Don't *brood* over a missed opportunity. Old English *brod* (hatching).

grist — D: Grain to be ground. Figuratively, something used to one's advantage; as, Prison was *grist* for the writer's novels. Old English *grindan* (to grind).

thrum — A: Play a stringed instrument, such as a guitar or banjo, in a monotonous or unskilful manner. Scottish and dialectal English.

rasp — D: Harsh, scraping sound such as that made by a file; as, The sergeant had an annoying *rasp* in his voice. Middle English *raspen* (to scrape together).

bleak — C: Dreary; without hope; as, a *bleak* future. Barren; as, a *bleak* landscape. Cold and cutting; as, *bleak* winter winds. Middle English *bleik* (pale).

wane — B: Decrease; grow gradually less; as, The school's good reputation began to *wane*. Old English *wanian*.

quail — B: Lose courage in the face of difficulty or danger; cower; as, The prisoner did not *quail* before his interrogators. Middle English *quailen* (to give way).

zeal — C: Fervour; intense, tireless and enthusiastic devotion to a cause or goal; as, the premier's *zeal* for a peace agreement. Middle English *zele*.

bane — D: Cause of misery, distress, harm or death; as, Crime is the *bane* of society. Old English *bana*.

gig — D: A short-term job, especially for a jazz musician; as, He played a *gig* last night at a hotel. Slang; origin unknown.

rime — A: Frost; feathery coating of ice formed when supercooled water droplets in fog hit an object that is also below freezing; as, The *rime* on the grass gave the garden a magical beauty. Old English *hrim* (frost).

fend — B: Repel; as, The corporation *fended* off the takeover attempt. Also, to manage, provide; as, The refugees *fended* for themselves. Middle English *fenden* (to defend).

preen — C: Dress up with fussy, painstaking care; as, She *preened* for hours before her date. Also, said of birds, to smooth or clean feathers with the beak. Middle English *preynen* (to prune).

cairn — D: Conical mound of stones set up as a marker; as, A *cairn* stood where the mountain climber had died. Gaelic *carn* (an elevation).

fell — A: Fierce; dreadful; cruel; as, a *fell* civil war. Also, devastatingly complete; as, He lost his house and his job in one *fell* swoop. Middle English *fel*.

Vocabulary Ratings
9 — 11 correct . . . Good
12 — 17 correct . . . Excellent
18 — 20 correct . . . Exceptional

MUTUALLY EXCLUSIVE

Definite maybe —Jon L. Runyan

Real phony —Gloria Schlesna

Strangely familiar —Jacqueline Schiff

 Light heavyweight —C. P. Miscavish

THE LONG AND SHORT

The "long and short" of this test—the sum and substance—is that half of the words are long and half have only one syllable. How many of these words do you know? Choose your answers; then turn the page to find your score.

bray — A: donkey cry. B: rough edge. C: barrier.
D: woven ornamental trimming.

ambulatory — A: without direction. B: seriously injured.
C: able to walk. D: energetic.

broach — A: introduce or mention. B: connect with.
C: disagree with. D: shock.

deferential — A: shy. B: without interest. C: mechanical.
D: respectful.

née — relating to A: place. B: birth name. C: size.
D: attitude.

manifestation — A: encounter. B: indication. C: strong inclination.
D: fullness.

snide — A: clever. B: malicious. C: abrupt. D: whispered.

heterogeneous — A: confusing. B: talented. C: congenial. D: varied.

lee — A: forefront. B: edge. C: shelter. D: bottom.

cartographer — A: disposal engineer. B: heart specialist.
C: astronomer. D: map-maker.

orb — A: piece of jewellery. B: historical find. C: computer term.
D: globe.

❝Discipline is remembering what you want.❞

—DAVID CAMPBELL

WIT BITS

Cheese grater: cheddar shredder —John Wood

Sore loser: bitter quitter —John Dratwa

Earthquake: chasm spasm —Ellis Stewart

---

intransigent — A: practical. B: uncompromising. C: not lasting.
   D: clairvoyant.
scam — A: swindle. B: outline. C: superficial examination.
   D: quick getaway.
acquiescence — A: greed. B: innocence. C: awareness.
   D: agreement.
wry — pertaining to A: meditative thought. B: sweet memory.
   C: facial expression. D: pain.
misapprehension — A: lack of fear. B: worry. C: unfair seizure.
   D: misunderstanding.
niche — A: cupboard. B: recess in a wall. C: noticeable scratch.
   D: interlocking part.
disingenuous — A: uncaring. B: clumsy. C: innocent.
   D: insincere.
splotch — A: small quantity. B: stain or spot. C: irregular pattern.
   D: descriptive sound.
blasphemous — A: slanderous. B: profane. C: angry. D: volatile.

66To have a right to do a thing is not at all the same
as to be right in doing it.**99**

—G. K. CHESTERTON

 *ANSWERS*

bray — A: Loud, harsh cry, as from a donkey. Old French *braire* (to cry out).

ambulatory — C: Able to walk about; as, an *ambulatory* patient. Also, pertaining to walking; as, *ambulatory* exercise. Latin *ambulare* (to walk).

broach — A: Introduce or mention a topic for discussion. Also, to tap or pierce a keg. Latin *broccus* (projecting).

deferential — D: Respectful; yielding to someone else's wishes or judgement; as, the student's *deferential* attitude towards his teacher. Latin *deferre* (to carry down).

née — B: Born; referring to the maiden name of a married woman; as, Mrs. Mary Lincoln, *née* Todd. French, from *naître* (to be born).

manifestation — B: Indication or evidence of the nature of a person or thing; as, The mechanic's repair was a *manifestation* of his skill. Latin *manifestus* (evident).

snide — B: Malicious; nasty; spiteful; as, The *snide* comment hurt her. Origin uncertain.

heterogeneous — D: Varied; consisting of unlike people or things; as, Most political parties are composed of *heterogeneous* personalities. Greek *hetero-* (other) and *genos* (kind, gender).

lee — C: Shelter or protection, especially from a storm; as, to crouch in the *lee* of a rock during a squall. Old English *hleo* (shelter).

cartographer — D: Someone who makes maps. French *carte* (map) and Greek *-graphia* (writing).

orb — D: Globe or sphere; as, the bright *orb* of the street lamp. Also, poetic description of a heavenly body. Latin *orbis* (circle).

intransigent — B: Uncompromising; stubbornly refusing to give up an outlook or position; as, The committee's *intransigent* policy created problems. Latin *in-* (not) and *transigere* (to agree).

scam — A: Swindle; dishonest scheme to make a quick profit; as, the horse-racing *scam* in the film *The Sting*. American slang; origin uncertain.

acquiescence — D: Agreement; acceptance; as, His *acquiescence* to her every wish. Latin *ad-* (at) and *quiescere* (to rest).

wry — C: Pertaining to anything twisted or distorted, especially a facial expression indicating displeasure or disgust; as, a *wry* smile. Also, ironic, perverse or mocking; as, *wry* humour. Old English *wrigian* (to turn).

misapprehension — D: Misunderstanding; mistaken idea; as, a *misapprehension* in negotiations between labour and management. English *mis-* (wrongly) and Latin *apprehendere* (to grasp).

niche — B: Recess in a wall for displaying an object. Also, figuratively, a position suitable for a person; as, She found her *niche* as a counsellor. French.

disingenuous — D: Insincere; deceitful; not straightforward; as, a *disingenuous* witness. Latin *dis-* (away from) and *ingenuus* (noble).

splotch — B: Stain; spot; as, an ugly *splotch* on the rug. Possibly a blend of *spot* and *blotch*.

blasphemous — B: Profane; showing disrespect for God or anything held sacred or in high esteem; as, a *blasphemous* book. Greek *blasphemos* (speaking evil).

Vocabulary Ratings

    9 — 11 correct ... Good
    12 — 17 correct ... Excellent
    18 — 20 correct ... Exceptional

66An invasion of armies can be resisted, but not an idea whose time has come.**99**

—VICTOR HUGO

COLOURFULLY COMMONPLACE

In your everyday vocabulary you have a variety of interesting words at hand that range from the commonplace to the colourfully technical. Mark the answer you think is correct and turn the page for your score.

swatch — A: a quick blow. B: petty theft. C: sample of cloth. D: repair of clothing.

linchpin — A: lapel jewellery. B: start-up computer switch. C: release mechanism. D: part of an axle.

console — A: support group. B: security blanket. C: marriage partner. D: cabinet.

coiffure — A: dress designer. B: hair style. C: silver service. D: curved railing.

ultraviolet — having A: short, invisible wavelengths. B: a bluish pigment. C: visible, long wavelengths. D: a deep-purple colour.

distaff — relating to A: helpers. B: women. C: distance. D: melancholy.

hidebound — A: tactless. B: leather-covered. C: tough. D: inflexible.

taproot — A: main plant root. B: engineering structure. C: dance with metal-tipped shoes. D: solution to a problem.

manger — A: feed box. B: bunk bed. C: dwelling. D: mattress.

highboy — A: chest of drawers. B: swindler. C: snob. D: chair for babies.

GOOD QUESTION!

Why is there a permanent press setting on most irons?

—Kay Mosure

How do you know when you've run out of invisible ink?

—Larry Andersen

---

condiment — A: candy. B: seasoning. C: combination.
    D: channel.

winnow — A: succeed. B: coax. C: separate. D: shrink from.

flange — A: hanging shelf. B: wedge. C: long, thin object.
    D: projecting rim or edge.

hutch — A: lake eel. B: tool-shed. C: window seat.
    D: pen for small animals.

trappings — A: sly tricks. B: accommodations.
    C: ornamental accessories. D: loose floorboards.

napery — A: soft, downy surface. B: Japanese sleeping mat.
    C: household linen. D: place of quiet.

aerate — A: lighten. B: expose to air. C: puff out.
    D: bring to public notice.

impeller — A: rotor blade. B: barrier. C: wrench. D: amplifier.

cloche — A: hose attachment. B: sundial. C: type of divider.
    D: bell-shaped cover.

fusion — A: a splitting apart. B: jumble or muddle. C: blending.
    D: warmth of feeling.

 *ANSWERS*

swatch — C: Sample of cloth; patch or characteristic specimen; as, to take home *swatches* of rugs for colour selection. Origin unknown.

linchpin — D: Axle pin that keeps a wheel in place; essential person or thing. Old English *lynis*.

console — D: Cabinet for radio, television, record player. Also, an ornamental bracket. French, from *consolateur* (a bracket in the shape of a carved figure).

coiffure — B: Style of hair arrangement; as, a *coiffure* of loose curls. Also, a headdress. French *coiffe* (cap).

ultraviolet — A: Having short wavelengths beyond the visible spectrum at the violet end; as, Sunlight's *ultraviolet* rays increase the risk of skin cancer. Latin *ultra-* (beyond) and English *violet*.

distaff — B: Relating to women or to maternal lineage; as, the *distaff* side of the Prime Minister's family. Old English *distaef* (a mechanism to hold wool for spinning).

hidebound — D: Inflexible and narrow-minded; locked into old customs and prejudices; as, a *hidebound* official. From the tightly stretched skin on starving cattle.

taproot — A: Main, vertical root from which others branch out. Metaphorically, anything that serves as a primary source of strength. Old English *taeappa* (tap).

manger — A: Feeding-trough for livestock; as, In the stable "she . . . laid him in a *manger* because there was no room for them in the inn." Old French *mangeoire*.

highboy — A: tall chest of drawers on legs.

condiment — B: A seasoning or sauce, such as pepper and mustard, that adds special flavour to food. Latin *condire* (to season).

winnow — C: Separate; sift the good from the bad; as, to *winnow* facts from rumours. Also, to throw grain into the breeze so that lighter chaff (husks) and dirt will blow away. Old English *windwian* (to fan).

flange — D: Projecting rim or edge, as on some window screens to hold them in place. Old French *flanche* (flank, side).

hutch — D: Pen or coop for small animals; also, a cupboard with open shelves on top to display objects. Old French *huche*.

trappings — C: Ornamental accessories; outward signs or indications. Old French *drap* (cloth).

napery — C: Household linen, such as napkins and tablecloths. Old French *nappe*.

aerate — B: Expose to air or cause air to circulate through; as, to *aerate* a reservoir's water supply by using fountains. Greek *aer* (air).

impeller — A: Rotor blade; device used to force a liquid along a pipe or move it within a closed area; as, a dishwasher's *impeller*. Latin *impellere* (to drive).

cloche — D: Bell-shaped glass cover for plants, food and the like. Also, closefitting woman's hat of the 1920s. French (bell).

fusion — C: A blending together; as, an athlete's *fusion* of speed and skill; also, the combining of two light nuclei to form a heavier nucleus with a loss of mass, which is converted into energy. Latin *fundere* (to melt).

Vocabulary Ratings
- 9 — 11 correct ... Good
- 12 — 17 correct ... Excellent
- 18 — 20 correct ... Exceptional

66I like trees because they seem more resigned to the way they have to live than other things do.**99**

—WILLA CATHER

MORE THAN MEETS THE EYE

Look-alikes can cause mistaken-identity problems among words as well as people. In this test you may find yourself hesitating over the meanings of the following paired words before finding the best answers. Turn the page to find out how you did.

affect — A: influence. B: plan. C: conclude. D: undertake.

effect — A: be the cause of. B: preclude. C: think up.
      D: adjust or control.

illicit — A: provocative. B: unlawful. C: secret. D: abnormal.

elicit — A: demand. B: evoke. C: break the law. D: ask for.

perimeter — A: proportion. B: territory. C: outer boundary.
      D: parade ground.

parameter — A: simultaneous occurrence. B: periphery.
      C: mathematical quantity. D: substitute.

classical — A: modern. B: outdated. C: remarkable.
      D: of Greek and Roman culture.

classic — A: up-to-date. B: timely. C: of the highest quality.
      D: old-fashioned.

evanescent — A: sparkling. B: fading quickly. C: colourful.
      D: flashing on and off.

effervescent — A: bubbling. B: crystal clear. C: momentary.
      D: lacking charisma.

MODIFIED MAXIMS

An ounce of pretension is worth a pound of manure.

—MARTHA SIMMONS

Caveman's motto: He who hesitates is lunch.

—STEPHEN C. LEAHY

Jockey's rule of thumb: Put your money where your mount is.

—PHYLLIS JEAN PORTER

> **"**What counts is not necessarily the size of the dog in the fight—it's the size of the fight in the dog.**"**
>
> —*DWIGHT D. EISENHOWER*

---

voracious — A: vicious. B: exciting. C: insatiable. D: truthful.

rapacious — A: evil. B: frightening. C: famished. D: greedy.

judicious — A: diplomatic. B: wise. C: watchful. D: legal.

judicial — A: ponderous. B: unbiased. C: sudden. D: prudent.

cynical — A: ill-tempered. B: disguising feelings.
C: contemptuously distrustful. D: reluctant to perform.

sceptical — A: dissenting. B: bigoted. C: heckling.
D: unconvinced.

obtuse — A: complicated. B: unreasonable. C: angular. D: dull.

abstruse — A: difficult to understand. B: unintelligent.
C: strangely different. D: straightforward.

queue — A: oval design. B: line of people. C: theory.
D: indication.

cue — A: indoor game. B: orderly formation. C: guiding suggestion.
D: solution.

INCREDIBLE EDIBLES

Bakery: "Cakes 66¢—Upside-down cakes 99¢"

—*SHARON FLYNN*

Fish Market: "Lox, stocked in barrel"

—*BRIAN S. HALL*

ANSWERS

affect — A: Influence; produce a response; as, People are deeply *affected* by Picasso's anti-war painting *Guernica*. Latin *afficere*.

effect — A: Be the cause of; bring about; as, to *effect* the unification of the two Germanys. Latin *efficere*.

illicit — B: Unlawful; unauthorised; as, Stock-exchange rules prohibit *illicit* trading in securities. Latin *illicitus*.

elicit — B: Evoke a response or reaction; draw out; as, The inquiry *elicited* important facts. Latin *elicere*.

perimeter — C: Outer boundary; as, We walked the *perimeter* of our farm. Greek *peri-* (around) and *metron* (measure).

parameter — C: Varying mathematical quantity whose values determine a system's form; as, death and survival *parameters* from insurance statistics. Informally, a guide; as, foreign-policy *parameters*. Latin *para-* (beside) and *metron*.

classical — D: Of Greek and Roman culture; as, a *classical* scholar. Also, traditional, as classical architecture or music. Latin *classicus* (superior).

classic — C: Of the highest quality; serving as a standard; as, Melville's *Moby Dick* is a *classic* American novel. Latin *classicus*.

evanescent — B: Fading quickly; barely perceptible; as, an *evanescent* dream. Latin *evanescere* (to vanish).

effervescent — A: Bubbling; as, an *effervescent* soft drink. Also, vivacious; as, an *effervescent* personality. Latin *effervescere* (to boil over).

voracious — C: Having an insatiable appetite for food or activity; as, a *voracious* reader of autobiographies. Latin *vorare* (to devour).

rapacious — D: Greedy; predatory; taking by force whatever one wants; as, a *rapacious* dictator. Latin *rapere* (to seize).

judicious — B: Wise; sensible; practical; as, *judicious* advice. Latin *judicium* (judgement).

judicial — B: Unbiased; fair; as, a *judicial* decision. Primarily of judges or a law court; as, the *judicial* system. Latin *judex* (judge).

cynical — C: Contemptuously distrustful; not believing in human goodness or sincerity. From the Cynics, ancient Greek philosophers thought of as self-righteous, misanthropic, even currish. Greek *kynos* (dog).

sceptical — D: Unconvinced; doubting; as, to be *sceptical* about a new medical cure. Greek *skeptikos* (reflective).

obtuse — D: Dull; insensitive; mentally slow; as, to be so *obtuse* as to ignore strong hints. Also, an angle greater than 90 degrees and less than 180. Latin *obtusus* (blunted).

abstruse — A: Difficult to understand; beyond average intelligence; as, an *abstruse* scientific concept. Latin *abstrudere* (to thrust away).

queue — B: Line of people waiting their turn. Also, a pigtail, or computer data "waiting in line" to be processed. Latin *cauda* (tail).

cue — C: Guiding suggestion; signal. Originally "Q" from Latin *quando* (when), written on scripts to indicate a character's entrance or action.

Vocabulary Ratings
9 — 11 correct . . . Good
12 — 17 correct . . . Excellent
18 — 20 correct . . . Exceptional

SPELLBOUND

I have a spelling checker,
It came with my PC;
It plainly marks four my revue
Mistakes I cannot sea.
I've run this poem threw it,
I'm sure your please too no,
Its letter perfect in it's weigh,
My checker tolled me sew.

—*Quoted by Pennye Harper*

This quiz contains a selection of "concept words"—expressions or phrases based on ideas and images. Concept words give us broader understanding and change the way we think and act. Try to catch the idea or image behind the following words. Turn the page to check your score.

anarchy — A: lawlessness. B: self-rule. C: mandate. D: ignorance.

networking — A: intense activism. B: development of contacts. C: illegal operation. D: projecting into outer space.

biodegradable — A: endangered. B: capable of decomposing. C: offensively odorous. D: polluting.

symbiosis — A: similarity. B: cure-all. C: close association. D: transformation.

ecumenical — A: helpful. B: relevant. C: universal. D: thrifty.

clone — A: joke. B: exclude. C: revitalise. D: duplicate.

feminism — doctrine pertaining to women's A: obligations. B: rights. C: femininity. D: inherent strength.

supply-side economics — theory that emphasises A: tax cuts. B: welfare. C: imports. D: exports.

black hole — A: moonless night. B: collapsed star. C: economic crisis. D: oceanic depression.

bluestocking — A: strongly religious woman. B: type of country music. C: high fashion. D: intellectual woman.

TAKE YOUR PIQUE

Courage: fear extinguisher —Ellis Stewart

Pessimist: one who no's too much —Franklin Krook

Smile: mirth mark —Daniel M. Evans

Boasting: patter of little feats —Marguerite Whitley May in
The Wall Street Journal

Grouch potato: TV addict who grumbles when disturbed

—Shelby Friedman in *Quote* magazine

Heir styling: genetic engineering —Al Bernstein

Befaxed: besieged by unsolicited fax messages

—Victor Navasky, quoted by William Grimes in *The New York Times*

---

populist — promoter of A: conformity. B: mainstream politics.
C: celebrities. D: the interests of ordinary people.

geopolitical — concerning A: local politics. B: the military.
C: politics and geography. D: nationalism.

relativity — theory concerning A: ethical judgements. B: family
trees. C: balance. D: matter, energy, time and space.

dystopia — A: wretched situation. B: place of magical charm.
C: superstitious belief. D: type of illness.

karma — A: unexplained event. B: illusion. C: love. D: fate.

byzantine — A: complex. B: peaceful. C: visionary.
D: seductive.

ergonomics — study of A: population. B: economic growth.
C: workplace design. D: industrial profits.

jihad — A: tribal custom. B: religious sect. C: jewel.
D: Islamic holy war.

philistine — A: uncultured person. B: foreigner.
C: one who is ingenious. D: selfish individual.

ecology — A: disease control. B: evolution. C: balance of nature.
D: heredity.

IN OTHER WORDS

Goblet: young turkey —Jerri L. Nunn
Physiology: science of carbonating soft drinks —Nathan Fabling
Counter-attack: January sales —G. Pearson

anarchy — A: Lawlessness; absence of government control resulting in political disorder and sometimes violence. Greek *anarchos* (without a leader).

networking — B: The development and maintenance of personal contacts for exchanging information on topics of mutual interest, such as careers.

biodegradable — B: Capable of decomposing into harmless products; as, a new generation of *biodegradable* plastics. Greek *bios* (life) and Late Latin *degradare* (to reduce the rank of).

symbiosis — C: Close association of two unlike organisms resulting in advantage to both; as, A *symbiosis* exists between the rhinoceros and the birds that eat annoying ticks on its back. Greek (a living together).

ecumenical — C: Universal; worldwide; specifically, relating to religious unity. Also, interdenominational; as, The *ecumenical* meeting represented all major religious faiths. Greek *oikoumenikos* (of the whole world).

clone — D: Duplicate; reproduce or propagate asexually. Also, copy a computer design under another brand name. Greek *klon* (a twig).

feminism — B: Doctrine based on the view that women should be given the rights, opportunities and treatment accorded to men. Latin *femina* (woman).

supply-side economics — A: Theory holding that the economy will be stimulated by investment incentives, such as tax cuts.

black hole — B: Perhaps the invisible remains of a collapsed star with a gravitational field so intense that neither matter nor light can escape.

bluestocking — D: A woman with strong intellectual ability and literary interests. From the *blue stockings* worn by a member of an 18th-century London literary society.

populist — D: Promoter of the interests of ordinary people, as opposed to the elite. Many politicians claim to be *populists*. Latin *populus* (people).

geopolitical — C: Concerning the interrelationship of politics and geography, especially as it affects a nation's foreign policies. From German *Geopolitik*.

relativity — D: Theory developed by Albert Einstein explaining, among other things, relationships among matter, energy, time and space.

dystopia — A: A hypothetical situation or place where everything is wretched and the people are miserable. The opposite of utopia; as, The tiny nation had become a *dystopia*. Greek *dys-* (bad) and *topos* (place).

karma — D: Fate. For Hindus and Buddhists, one's actions bring inevitable results, good or bad, either in this life or in a reincarnation. Sanskrit (deed, act).

byzantine — A: Complex, devious and scheming; resembling the policies of the ancient Byzantine Empire.

ergonomics — C: Study of workplace and equipment designed to eliminate discomfort and fatigue. Greek *ergon* (work) and *-nomy* (arrangement, management).

jihad — D: Islamic holy war against unbelievers or enemies, undertaken as a religious duty. Arabic.

philistine — A: Uncultured, materialistic person with little interest in the arts. From Philistine, warlike inhabitant of ancient coastal Palestine.

ecology — C: Balance of nature; study of the interrelationship of organisms and their environment. Greek *oikos* (habitat) and *-logy* (study of).

Vocabulary Ratings

     9 — 11 correct ... Good
     12 — 17 correct ... Excellent
     18 — 20 correct ... Exceptional

PROFITS WITH INTEREST

Words are assets you can bank on. Use the following list to see if you make a verbal profit. Turn the page to get to the bottom line.

naïve — A: refreshingly direct. B: reserved and cool. C: unsophisticated. D: carefree.

dilemma — A: catastrophe. B: reluctance to act. C: perplexing situation. D: desperation.

serape — A: blanket used as a poncho. B: sharp reply. C: brief rest. D: carrying case.

retrograde — A: backwards. B: smooth. C: level. D: advanced.

fiat — A: technological feat. B: arbitrary decree. C: power. D: culmination.

montage — A: large screen. B: actor's monologue. C: elongated balcony. D: composite picture.

adept — A: confident. B: quick. C: skilful. D: effortless.

immemorial — A: complimentary. B: ancient. C: unremarkable. D: not to be forgotten.

mollify — A: pacify. B: disguise. C: gladden. D: enhance.

recount — A: be long-winded. B: synthesise. C: ignore. D: tell in detail.

QUIP WITS

One day I called my broker about a stock that had been down in the dumps. "Do you think I'll live to see it go higher?" I asked. "Frankly," he said, "I wish you were a younger man."

—CONTRIBUTED BY DONALD S. REISS

coin — A: evaluate anew. B: imitate. C: invent. D: abscond.

indiscreet — A: unwise. B: confused. C: humorously inconsistent.
D: frenzied.

attest — A: challenge. B: depend on. C: confirm. D: qualify.

variance — A: congruence. B: comparison. C: flexibility.
D: difference.

minatory — A: pertaining to fish. B: threatening. C: insignificant.
D: haughty.

frugal — A: quiet. B: obstinate. C: efficient. D: thrifty.

precept — A: feeling or prediction. B: legal decision.
C: rule of conduct. D: idea.

surcease — A: lengthy explanation. B: cessation. C: something
added. D: extreme situation.

homily — A: sermon. B: pithy saying. C: peaceful atmosphere.
D: epic poem.

preternatural — A: primitive. B: supernatural. C: spontaneous.
D: artificial.

MAKING ALLOWANCES

To make the kids do what we want

We must be real inventive;

In Grandma's day 'twas called a bribe

Today it's an incentive.

—JUDI O'SULLIVAN

ANSWERS

naïve — C: Unsophisticated; simple; innocent. French, from *naïf* (natural).

dilemma — C: Perplexing, unavoidable situation in which a choice must be made between two equally undesirable alternatives. Greek *di-* (two) and *lemma* (proposition).

serape — A: Woollen blanket used as an outer garment in Latin America, especially Mexico. From Mexican Spanish.

retrograde — A: Backward; as, The planet exhibited *retrograde* motion through the constellations. Latin *retro-* (backward) and *gradi* (to walk).

fiat — B: Arbitrary decree; authoritative order; as, The tyrant's *fiat* sent troops into a neighbouring country. Latin (let it be done).

montage — D: Composite picture made by superimposing one element on another; as, a *montage* of notables. French, from *monter* (to mount).

adept — C: Skilful; proficient; as, The older couples were *adept* dancers. Latin *adipisci* (to attain).

immemorial — B: Ancient; beyond memory or record; as, The sexes have been battling since time *immemorial*. Latin *in-* (without) and *memoria* (memory).

mollify — A: Pacify; soothe; as, to *mollify* an angry customer. Latin *mollis* (soft).

recount — D: Tell in detail; give a full account of; as, Our daughter and her husband *recounted* their diving experience near a killer whale. French *re-* (again) and *conter* (to relate).

coin — C: Invent a word or phrase; as, Our friend *coined* "flustrated" to express flustered frustration. Old French *coign* (metal stamp).

indiscreet — A: Unwise; lacking good judgement; thoughtless; as, Blurting out a secret is *indiscreet*. Latin *indiscretus* (unseparated).

attest — C: Confirm; declare to be genuine; as, The students' test scores *attest* to their teacher's skill. Latin *attestari* (to bear witness).

variance — D: Difference; deviation; as, a *variance* between two accounts of the game. Also, permission to bypass certain regulations. Latin *variare* (to vary, alter).

minatory — B: Threatening; menacing; as, a *minatory* forecast of violent thunderstorms. Latin *minari* (to threaten).

frugal — D: Thrifty; not wasteful; as, My *frugal* grandmother kept odds and ends of threads for a rainy day. Latin *frux* (profit).

precept — C: Rule or guiding principle of conduct; as, The *precept* "waste not, want not" takes on new meaning. Latin *prae-* (before) and *capere* (to take).

surcease — B: Cessation; as, Sometimes we need *surcease* from the many issues vying for our attention. French *surseoir* (to suspend).

homily — A: Sermon or discourse on a moral or religious topic. Greek *homilos* (assembly).

preternatural — B: Supernatural; beyond what is normal; as, With *preternatural* strength she freed her husband, who was pinned under the car. Latin *praeternaturalis*.

Vocabulary Ratings
    9 — 11 correct . . . Good
    12 — 17 correct . . . Excellent
    18 — 20 correct . . . Exceptional

66There are no shortcuts to any place worth going.**99**

—*BEVERLY SILLS*

BIG BANGS

Don't miss the chance to put a big bang in your conversation with strong, effective words like those listed below. How many of them do you know? Turn the page to find your score.

acumen — A: exactness. B: potential. C: shrewdness.
D: assurance.

premonition — A: understanding. B: forewarning.
C: determination. D: mistrust.

criterion — A: explanation. B: essence. C: standard.
D: turning point.

parlous — A: exceedingly polite. B: timid. C: talkative.
D: dangerous.

extricate — A: frustrate. B: isolate. C: get rid of. D: set free.

myriad — A: assorted. B: colourful. C: vast in number.
D: demanding.

analogue — A: detailed analysis. B: something similar.
C: chronological record. D: something opposite.

picayune — A: trivial. B: peculiar. C: adventurous.
D: fussy.

adage — A: advantage. B: wise elder. C: enlargement.
D: proverb.

behest — A: something handed down. B: equality. C: good turn.
D: urgent request.

66The kind of humour I like is the thing that makes me laugh for five seconds and think for ten minutes.**99**

—WILLIAM DAVIS

66Talent is a flame. Genius is a fire.**99**

—BERN WILLIAMS

---

cobble — A: hinder. B: strike out. C: make hastily. D: withdraw.

vintage — A: outdated. B: classic or characteristic. C: traditionally suitable. D: ingenious.

segment — A: arc. B: solid residue. C: classification. D: section.

torpid — A: hot and heavy. B: rapid. C: sluggish. D: dangerous.

penultimate — A: next to last. B: opposing. C: extreme. D: finest.

viability — A: availability. B: effectiveness. C: rationality. D: qualification.

emblematic — A: symbolic. B: decorated. C: carefully outlined. D: significant.

roil — A: clarify. B: wrap around. C: make muddy. D: detonate.

infallible — A: obnoxiously confident. B: very stubborn. C: unbelievable. D: absolutely trustworthy.

crescendo — A: wavy motion. B: gradual increase. C: shrillness. D: decreasing pace.

DEFINE POINTS

Rare book: One that comes back after you've lent it.

—A. BRAITHWAITE

 ANSWERS

acumen — C: Shrewdness; keenness and insight in understanding and handling practical affairs; as, having financial *acumen*. Latin *acuere* (to sharpen).

premonition — B: Forewarning; hunch something bad may happen; as, The mother's *premonition* of danger saved her daughter. Latin *praemonere* (to warn beforehand).

criterion — C: Standard or rule for evaluating something; as, a *criterion* for employment. Greek *kriterion* (means of judging).

parlous — D: Dangerous; risky; perilous; as, The ravaged nation is in *parlous* condition. Middle English contraction of *perilous*.

extricate — D: Set free from a difficulty; disentangle; as, to *extricate* oneself from an embarrassing situation. Latin *extricare*.

myriad — C: Vast in number; innumerable; as, *myriad* requests for assistance. Greek *myriados* (ten thousand).

analogue — B: Something similar; as, There is no *analogue* for the rapid world changes we are witnessing today. Greek *analogos* (in proportion).

picayune — A: Trivial; trifling; of small importance; as, He doesn't fuss over *picayune* details. Louisiana French *picaillon* (small coin).

adage — D: Proverb; traditional, popular saying expressing a general truth; as, the old *adage* "Live and let live." Latin *adagium*, related to *aio* (I say).

behest — D: Urgent request; command; as, at the *behest* of the President. Old English *behaes* (vow).

cobble — C: Make or compose in a hasty or clumsy way; as, The small country *cobbled* together a temporary survival programme. From *cobbler*.

vintage — B: Classic; characteristic of a particular era; as, The dress code was *vintage* 1960s. Also, produced in a particular wine year. Latin *vinum* (wine).

segment — D: One of the sections or parts into which something can be separated; as, *segments* of an insect's body. Latin *secare* (to cut).

torpid — C: Sluggish; slow; apathetic; dull; as, the committee's *torpid* indifference to the request. Latin *torpere* (to be numb, inert).

penultimate — A: Next to last; as, The *penultimate* scene was the most moving in the play. Latin *paene* (almost) and *ultimus* (last).

viability — B: Effectiveness; ability to succeed or survive; as, The senator wanted to retain her political *viability*. Latin *vita* (life).

emblematic — A: Symbolic; serving as an emblem; as, The monetary conference is *emblematic* of international co-operation. Greek *emblema* (raised ornament).

roil — C: Make muddy by stirring up sediment; hence, also, to irritate, make angry; as, She did not allow herself to be *roiled* by his remarks. Old French *rouil* (rust, mud).

infallible — D: Absolutely trustworthy; never failing; unerring; as, an *infallible* remedy, guide or memory. Latin *infallibilis*.

crescendo — B: Gradual increase in loudness or intensity; as, the *crescendo* of fierce winds. Latin *crescere* (to arise, grow).

Vocabulary Ratings
> 9 — 11 correct . . . Good
> 12 — 17 correct . . . Excellent
> 18 — 20 correct . . . Exceptional

FIREWORKS

Fabulous yellow
Roman candles exploding
Like spiders across the stars
And in the middle you see
The blue centrelight pop
And everybody goes "Awww!"

—JACK KEROUAC

THINK AGAIN

The English language has some confusing rules of pronunciation. Consider such look-alike words as though, bough *and* enough, *and the fact that sometimes there are several meanings for words that sound the same. Do you know the meanings of the following, sometimes tricky words? Turn the page to find your score.*

gnarled — A: carelessly thrown together. B: having knobby lumps. C: smooth. D: hacked up.

fjord — A: snow-covered mountain. B: narrow inlet between cliffs. C: musical instrument. D: Norwegian folk tale.

timbre — A: characteristic tone. B: particular rhythm. C: construction material. D: tensile strength.

rancour — A: despair. B: disillusionment. C: jubilation. D: resentment.

aegis — A: protection. B: dramatic poem. C: channel. D: framework.

berserk — A: awkward. B: odd. C: frenzied. D: careless.

comparable — A: greater. B: clear. C: less. D: similar.

dais — A: receptacle for flowers. B: platform for speakers. C: reading desk. D: front of a building.

germane — A: graceful. B: relevant. C: harmonious. D: illusory.

kudos — A: Oriental martial art. B: African animal. C: praise. D: massage.

unctuous — A: contented to a fault. B: kindly and caring. C: pretending sincerity. D: perfumed.

WRONG MOTS

"Today we learned the Heimlich remover."

—Quoted by Lynith G. Brown

66When my class came indoors after playing, I noticed that one boy had a red mark around his neck. It had been caused, he explained, when his scarf was pulled off his neck. Quite impressed with the injury, he exclaimed, 'I was almost decaffeinated!'**99**

—KIM HERR

---

vignette — A: sauce or dressing. B: small eyeglasses. C: delicate vase. D: short description.

docile — A: peaceful. B: amorous. C: ineffectual. D: submissive.

onus — A: singleness of purpose. B: prophetic sign. C: burden. D: obstacle.

patina — A: outside dining area. B: surface film. C: dialect. D: scatter rug.

vagary — A: contrariness. B: irritating slowness. C: whim. D: fuzzy thought.

critique — A: detailed summary. B: severe scolding. C: irrefutable proof. D: thorough evaluation.

essay — A: try. B: resign. C: divert. D: suggest.

prescient — A: primitive. B: obtuse. C: having an inkling of future events. D: bright and cheerful.

pseudonym — A: fictitious name. B: dietary supplement. C: subtle lie. D: secret message.

SEUDONYM

 ANSWERS

gnarled — B: Having knobby lumps; twisted, bent; as a *gnarled* tree trunk. Middle English *knor* (a swelling).

fjord — B: Long, narrow, deep inlet from the sea between cliffs, as in Norway. Old Icelandic *fjordhr*.

timbre — A: Characteristic tone; distinctive quality of a voice or an instrument; as, the sweet *timbre* of her voice. Old French (a kind of drum).

rancour — D: Bitter, long-lasting resentment or hatred; as the *rancour* Croatian and Serbian troops felt for each other. Latin *rancere* (to stink, be rancid).

aegis — A: Protection; as, relief supplies sent under the *aegis* of the United Nations. Also, sponsorship. Greek *aigis* (shield).

berserk — C: Frenzied and emotionally upset to a violent extent; as, Teased mercilessly, the dog went *berserk*. Old Icelandic *berserkr* (wild warrior in a bearskin).

comparable — D: Similar; equivalent; as, The two nations have *comparable* regimes. Latin *com-* (together) and *par* (equal).

dais — B: Raised platform for speakers or guests of honour. Middle English *deis* (high table in a hall).

germane — B: Relevant; appropriate or fitting; as, arguments *germane* to the issue. Latin *germanus* (having the same parents).

kudos — C: Praise, honour or acclaim for achievement; as, The teacher deserved her *kudos*. Greek *kydos* (glory or fame).

unctuous — C: Pretending sincerity with a smug or virtuous demeanour, often with an oily charm; as, an *unctuous* con artist. Latin *ungere* (to anoint).

vignette — D: Short, graceful description or memorable scene; as, character *vignettes* in a film. Also, decorative design or a picture with no definite edge. French *vigne* (vine).

docile — **D:** Submissive; easy to manage or discipline; as, a *docile* pony. Latin *docere* (to teach).

onus — **C:** Difficult burden or responsibility that may cause anxiety or hardship; blame; as, the *onus* of making a life-and-death decision. Latin.

patina — **B:** Surface film produced by age or use; greenish incrustation on copper or bronze. Italian (tarnish).

vagary — **C:** Whim; unpredictable, often irresponsible, act or idea; as, the *vagaries* of fate. Latin *vagari* (to wander).

critique — **D:** Thorough evaluation, particularly of a work of art or literature. Greek *kritikos* (able to discern).

essay — **A:** Try, especially a difficult task; as, to *essay* a new beginning in a science-fiction story. Old French *essai* (trial).

prescient — **C:** Having an inkling of future events; as, a *prescient* economist. Latin *praescire* (to know beforehand).

pseudonym — **A:** Fictitious name taken by a writer; as, John Le Carré is the *pseudonym* of English author David John Moore Cornwell. Greek *pseudo* (false) and *onyma* (name).

Vocabulary Ratings
      9 — 11 correct ... Good
      12 — 17 correct ... Excellent
      18 — 20 correct ... Exceptional

FRACTURED PHRASES
"I think his wife would leave him at the slightest prevarication."

—John Scott Fones

HIDDEN MEANINGS

Digging out the definition of each word you're curious about is a good way to "bone up" on your vocabulary. Test yourself against this list of colourful, exotic and practical words. Then turn the page to find your results.

seascape — A: wave top. B: ocean debris. C: picture. D: boating accident.

aficionado — A: expert. B: good friend. C: guide. D: ardent fan.

facsimile — A: fake. B: model or example. C: nostrum. D: exact copy.

implode — A: load. B: burst inwards. C: laminate. D: instigate to action.

impresario — A: magician. B: mountebank. C: manager. D: impersonator.

barrio — A: leather thong. B: Spanish-American food. C: Spanish-speaking neighbourhood. D: horse-training corral.

indelible — A: permanent. B: beyond doubt. C: impenetrable. D: eradicable.

inveigle — A: complicate. B: entice. C: break into. D: denounce.

marauding — A: parading. B: wandering aimlessly. C: brawling. D: raiding.

database — A: starting point. B: system of signals. C: collection of information. D: domicile.

ROUNDABOUTS

Double occupancy means two can stay as cheaply as one who has to pay double if he's alone. —Ralph Shaffer

ensemble — A: sacred music. B: old-fashioned dance. C: musical fanfare. D: group of performers.

commodious — A: spacious. B: sheltering. C: well-supplied. D: comfortable.

stymie — A: hinder. B: stimulate. C: confuse. D: disgrace.

flair — A: emergency signal. B: enthusiasm. C: lighthearted bravado. D: natural ability.

replete — A: embellished. B: reworked. C: abounding. D: lacking energy.

genial — A: spontaneous. B: kindly. C: fascinating. D: ingratiating.

communiqué — A: propaganda. B: cipher. C: announcement. D: indiscretion.

slough — A: botch. B: ignore. C: slouch. D: shed.

retaliation — A: keeping score. B: repayment in kind. C: open disrespect. D: long-lasting hatred.

militant — A: aggressive. B: opinionated. C: practical. D: organised.

FEAR ITSELF
Fobia: fear of misspelled words —Charles Burgess
Hype-ochondria: fear of TV commercials —Jacqueline Schiff
Tripidation: fear of travelling —Hank Billings
Auldlanxiety: fear of New Year's Eve —Bonnie Pastoor

 *ANSWERS*

seascape — C: Picture, sketch, painting or photograph of the sea; as, The artist Winslow Homer was noted for his *seascapes*. Variation of *landscape*.

aficionado — D: Ardent fan, supporter or devotee; as, a crossword-puzzle *aficionado*. Spanish *aficionar* (to arouse affection).

facsimile — D: Exact copy or reproduction. Also, method of transmitting graphic matter electronically by telephone line. Latin *fac simile* (to make similar).

implode — B: To burst or collapse violently inwards; as, The robot submarine *imploded* and sank. Latin *in-* (in, within) and *plaudere* (to clap, beat or stamp).

impresario — C: Manager, producer or organiser of public entertainment, especially concerts, opera or ballet. Italian *imprendere* (to undertake).

barrio — C: Spanish-speaking neighbourhood. In Hispanic countries, a district or suburb of a city. Arabic *barr* (open area).

indelible — A: Permanent; incapable of being erased or removed; as, *indelible* ink. Also, unforgettable; as, *indelible* memories. Latin *indelebilis* (indestructible).

inveigle — B: Entice or persuade by trickery or cleverness; tempt; as, to *inveigle* someone into a bad investment. Middle French *aveugler* (to delude, make blind).

marauding — D: Raiding and ravaging an area in search of plunder and the like; as, *marauding* troops. French *maraud* (rascal, tomcat).

database — C: Comprehensive collection of electronic information designed for quick computerised retrieval and updating; as, a *database* of potential customers' names.

ensemble — D: Group of entertainers who perform together; as, a brass *ensemble*. Also, term for a well-matched outfit of clothes. Late Latin *insimul* (at the same time).

commodious — A: Spacious and roomy; as, to hold the meeting in the *commodious* old ballroom. Latin *commodus* (convenient).

stymie — A: Hinder or thwart; as, The recession *stymied* economic growth. Scottish origin.

flair — D: Natural ability, talent or knack; as, the columnist's *flair* for the apt word. Also, stylishness; as, to dress with *flair*. Old French *flairer* (to give off an odour or scent).

replete — C: Abounding; plentifully supplied; as, a resort *replete* with night life, sports and good food. Also, gorged or sated. Latin *replere* (to fill up).

genial — B: Kindly, pleasant and cheerful; as, *genial* grandparents. Latin *genius* (guardian, deity).

communiqué — C: Announcement; official communication or bulletin reporting an event; as, A *communiqué* was issued after the summit meeting. From French *communiquer* (to inform).

slough — D: Shed; get rid or dispose of; cast off; as, At ease now, she *sloughed* off her fears. German *Schlauch* (a skin).

retaliation — B: Repayment in kind, especially for a wrong or an injury; a getting even; as, Martin Luther King, Jr., encouraged love, not *retaliation*. Latin *retaliare*.

militant — A: Aggressive and vigorous in support of a cause; as, a *militant* political activist. Also, warlike. Latin *militare* (to serve as a soldier).

Vocabulary Ratings

       9 — 11 correct . . . Good
     12 — 17 correct . . . Excellent
     18 — 20 correct . . . Exceptional

66Vision is the art of seeing things invisible.**99**

—JONATHAN SWIFT

Here's a collection of words taken from several cross-word puzzles and brain-teasers. Match wits with the puzzle constructors and select the answer you think is correct. Turn the page for your score.

pomp — A: self-assurance. B: fame. C: stately display. D: upswept hair style.

guru — A: African antelope. B: spiritual adviser. C: gifted person. D: deceptive gambler.

retrench — A: establish. B: economise. C: dig out. D: fill in with earth.

précis — A: summary. B: correct method. C: advance showing. D: prediction.

modish — A: fashionable. B: temperamental. C: snobbish. D: shy.

ilk — A: source. B: sickness. C: small group. D: same kind.

medley — A: recurring theme. B: assortment of items. C: average result. D: softness.

allay — A: join. B: state to be true. C: calm. D: retreat from.

prevail — A: beg. B: prevent. C: grasp. D: triumph.

dam — A: woman of nobility. B: great strength. C: animal's female parent. D: counteraction.

askance — with A: horror. B: suspicion. C: awkwardness. D: coyness.

❝The world's major trouble spots these days were formerly known only to crossword-puzzle fans.**❞**

—Val Tupy, quoted by Jack Rosenbaum in San Francisco Independent

Wɪᴛ Bɪᴛꜱ

Kids' bedtime: pyjama drama —Connie Theis

Fast-food restaurant: economy gastronomy —David E. Reilly

Proofreader: blooper snooper —Doreen Clendenen

---

tinge — A: burn. B: make a light, ringing sound.
    C: colour slightly. D: spoil or corrupt.
wan — A: pale. B: tender. C: unexpressive. D: thin.
bauble — A: foolish talk. B: small bubble. C: social error.
    D: worthless trinket.
par — A: superior attainment. B: figure of speech. C: smallness.
    D: average condition.
prig — person who is A: boring. B: self-righteous. C: gossipy.
    D: witty.
riff — A: animation. B: rupture of a relationship.
    C: disreputable person. D: repeated melodic phrase.
downy — A: soft and fluffy. B: foolish and flighty.
    C: somewhat seedy. D: languid or flabby.
mote — A: wide ditch. B: emotional outburst. C: speck.
    D: act of shedding.
lulu — A: Polynesian feast. B: euphemism for washroom.
    C: lucky break. D: anything remarkable.

CAUGHT IN THE RIDDLE

Q: What do you get when you cross the language barrier?

A: A phonic boom.

—Mᴏʀʀɪꜱ G. Hᴜʟᴛꜱ

pomp — C: Stately display. Also, ostentatious showiness. Greek *pompe* (solemn procession).

guru — B: Spiritual adviser, teacher or highly regarded leader (sometimes used derisively); as, a literary *guru*. Sanskrit (weighty, venerable).

retrench — B: Economise; reduce or curtail expenses. Old French *re-* (back) and *trenchier* (to cut).

précis — A: Concise summary of the essentials; as, a *précis* of one's employment background. Latin *praecidere* (to shorten).

modish — A: Fashionable; in the latest style; trendy; as, *modish* jewellery. French *mode* (fashion, vogue) and English *-ish* (pertaining to).

ilk — D: The same kind, sort, class. Often used in a belittling sense; as, Imagine inviting people of that *ilk*! Old English *ilca* (same).

medley — B: Assortment of unrelated items; hodgepodge. Old French *medlee*.

allay — C: Calm or quiet fears or anger; as, to *allay* the dread of being abandoned. Old English *alecgan* (to put down).

prevail — D: Triumph; dominate; as, She *prevailed* against all odds. Also, to be widespread; as, Happiness *prevailed*. Or, to use persuasion successfully; as, He *prevailed* upon us to go. Latin *praevalere* (to be stronger).

dam — C: Female parent of any four-legged animal, especially domestic animals; as, the famous *dam* of a champion thoroughbred horse. Thirteenth-century variation of *dame*.

askance — B: With suspicion, mistrust, disapproval; as, She looked *askance* at the huckster. Also, a sideways glance. Middle English *ascaunce* (as if).

tinge — C: Colour slightly; as, a sunset *tinged* with pink. Also, to add a trace; as, joy *tinged* with regret. Latin *tingere*.

wan — A: Pale, from illness, exhaustion or deep unhappiness; as, her *wan*, haggard face. Old English *wann* (dark, gloomy).

bauble — D: Worthless, showy trinket; any useless thing; as, *baubles* wrapped in expensive-looking boxes. Old French *baubel* (toy).

par — D: Average or normal condition; as, feeling up to *par*. Also, face value of bonds, etc.; standard for golf strokes; an equal footing; as, on a *par* with one's peers. Latin (equal).

prig — B: Person who is self-righteous or smug about assumed superior virtues and wisdom. British slang; origin unknown.

riff — D: In jazz, a repeated melodic phrase as a background accompaniment for a soloist. Probably from *refrain*.

downy — A: Soft and fluffy; as, a *downy* pillow. From English *down* (young duck's feathers).

mote — C: Speck or particle; as, "And why beholdest thou the *mote* that is in thy brother's eye, but considerest not the beam that is in thine own eye?" Old English *mot*.

lulu — D: Anyone or anything remarkable or outstanding, as a beautiful girl, windstorm, examination and the like. U.S. slang, probably from the nickname for *Louise*.

Vocabulary Ratings
> 9 — 11 correct . . . Good
> 12 — 17 correct . . . Excellent
> 18 — 20 correct . . . Exceptional

COLLECTIVELY SPEAKING

A raft of survivors —Larry Mills

A drove of cars —Ruth Ann Esch

A pound of hammers —Louis Phillips

WORDPLAY

Wordplay can be endlessly fascinating. For example, in this quiz of paired words, when you substitute just one letter for another, you end up with an entirely new word. Choose the meaning you think is correct for each. Turn the page for your score.

sear — A: insult. B: thirst. C: predict. D: scorch.

seer — A: elderly person. B: cooking utensil. C: idealist. D: prophet.

dun — A: soil. B: add to. C: demand payment. D: find fault.

don — A: chaperone. B: put on. C: give. D: lord over.

nib — A: point. B: small amount. C: essence. D: clever response.

nub — A: clumsy person. B: lack of courtesy. C: mechanical fitting. D: knob or lump.

vie — A: long for. B: compete. C: urge. D: pass through.

via — A: over. B: towards. C: by way of. D: between.

quark — A: in physics, a fundamental particle. B: unusual star. C: newt. D: any unexplained phenomenon.

quirk — A: dagger. B: self-satisfied smile. C: odd mannerism. D: habit.

couch — A: camouflage. B: put into words. C: relax. D: hunker down.

NINETIES NOMENCLATURE

Shamnesia: fake memory lapse —Ellis Stewart

Slugvest: bulletproof jacket —B. J. Thompson

Ecomaniac: environmental activist —Wesley G. Hunt

WORRY WORDS

Hamnesia: bad actor's memory lapse —Shelby Friedman

Angoraphobia: fear of fluffy sweaters —Brian Todd Simmons

Fee-fie-fo-bia: fear of giants —Virginia Ebright

---

conch — A: part of a saddle. B: crown. C: rope. D: shell.

wax — A: begin. B: diminish. C: melt. D: grow.

wag — A: sprite. B: dishonest person. C: joker. D: someone who is ineffectual.

score — A: criticise severely. B: cleanse. C: flatter. D: treat with deference.

scope — A: agenda. B: range or extent. C: educated guess. D: conclusion.

rife — A: divided. B: petty. C: widespread. D: accurate.

rile — A: enliven. B: waste time. C: blunder. D: annoy.

chafe — A: rub against. B: tease. C: cut through. D: challenge persistently.

chape — A: compost. B: belt loop. C: grain husks. D: foolishness.

WHAT DO YOU CALL . . .

. . . the guy who understands everything you say? Roger

—Joseph P. Lassegard

. . . the fellow you find lying on your porch? Matt

—Janet Blamford

. . . the woman who never stands up straight? Eileen

—John Lynch

 *ANSWERS*

sear — D: Scorch; brown quickly; wither; as, The summer sun can *sear* a field. Old English *searian* (to dry).

seer — D: Prophet; one who predicts; wise person; someone with deep moral and spiritual insight. Middle English *seen* (to see).

dun — C: Demand payment of a debt; as, Credit-card companies *dun* delinquent customers. Perhaps derived from Joe Dun, a sixteenth-century London debt collector.

don — B: Put on; as, They quickly *donned* raincoats and left. Contraction of *do* and *on*.

nib — A: Point of anything; as, the *nib* of a pen; the diamond *nib* of a record player. Old English *nebb* (beak).

nub — D: Knob or lump. Also, the gist or heart of the matter; as, the *nub* of a discussion. Middle Low German *knubbe* (knot).

vie — B: Compete; struggle for superiority; as, tennis rivals *vying* for a championship. Old French *envier* (to challenge).

via — C: By way of; through; as, to go from Montreal to Sydney *via* Hawaii. Also, by means of; as, *via* airmail. Latin.

quark — A: In physics, a fundamental particle of which protons and neutrons are made. Coined from a line in James Joyce's *Finnegans Wake*: "Three *quarks* for Muster Mark."

quirk — C: Odd mannerism or trait; idiosyncrasy; as, her *quirk* of talking to house plants. Also, sudden change or twist; as, to win by a *quirk* of fate. Origin unknown.

couch — B: Put into words; express; as, She *couched* her request in an amusing way. Old French *coucher* (to lay down).

conch — D: Large, spiral shell of various marine molluscs. Greek *konche*.

wax — D: Grow, as said of the moon. Also, to increase in intensity; as, to *wax* enthusiastic over an idea. Old English *weaxan*.

wag — C: Joker; wisecracker; wit. Perhaps shortened from Middle English *waghalter* (rogue, rascal or mischievous person; also, someone likely to hang).

score — A: Criticise severely; berate; as, The media *scored* the politician's poor judgement. Old Norse *skora* (to notch).

scope — B: Range or extent; as, within the *scope* of his ability. Also, opportunity; as, the exciting *scope* of the plan. Greek *scopos* (aim, target).

rife — C: Widespread, suggesting an increase of something; as, a city *rife* with drug-related crime. Old English *ryfe* (abundant).

rile — D: Annoy; vex; irk; as, People were *riled* over the unexpected increase in taxes. Variation of *roil* (to stir up).

chafe — A: Rub against, making sore or worn; as, The stiff collar *chafed* her neck. Also, to become impatient; as, He *chafed* at restrictions. Middle English *chaufen* (to warm).

chape — B: A sliding loop on a belt or strap; also, the metal cap of a scabbard-point. Late Latin *cappa* (head covering).

Vocabulary Ratings
9 — 11 correct . . . Good
12 — 17 correct . . . Excellent
18 — 20 correct . . . Exceptional

WOULD YOU SAY THAT . . .

. . . people who sell perfume are always sticking their business in your nose? —Ink Inc.

. . . the U.S. trade deficit is news of considerable import?
—Bill Tammeus in *The Kansas City Star*

Few mystery writers use vocabulary with greater skill than P. D. James. The following words are taken from her book 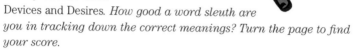 Devices and Desires. *How good a word sleuth are you in tracking down the correct meanings? Turn the page to find your score.*

pallid — A: gloomy or sad. B: smooth and glowing.
    C: lacking colour. D: submissive.

cumbersome — A: obnoxious. B: sluggish. C: unwieldy.
    D: diminutive.

raucous — A: piercing. B: undercooked. C: loud and harsh.
    D: vulgar.

cursory — A: obscene. B: crafty. C: mean. D: superficial.

clutch — A: cluster. B: keyhole. C: obvious clue. D: small cage.

concomitant — A: resulting. B: occurring together.
    C: fully committed. D: understandable.

reticent — A: pure. B: furtive. C: reserved. D: effusive.

condolences — A: congratulations. B: expressions of sympathy.
    C: words of forgiveness. D: acts of conciliation.

ostensibly — A: virtually. B: obviously. C: strictly.
    D: apparently.

sobriquet — A: actress in a light comedy. B: witty remark.
    C: type of painting. D: nickname.

WORDS TO THE WISE

Murder mysteries in print, like crossword puzzles and chocolate, are little getaways of certainty and comfort.

—JOHN DOUGLAS, QUOTED BY AMY CLYDE IN THE NEW YORK TIMES

CAUGHT IN THE RIDDLE

Q: Why is a good writer like a criminal?

A: Because they both prefer short sentences.

—RICHARD CRASTA

---

lugubrious — A: mournful. B: greasy. C: fawning.
D: slow and heavy.

frisson — A: shudder. B: calm. C: decorative border.
D: type of dessert.

venue — A: recollection. B: meeting place. C: passageway.
D: long vista.

recrimination — A: setback. B: rebirth. C: countercharge.
D: asperity.

vicarious — A: many and varied. B: doubtful. C: transitory.
D: serving as a substitute.

histrionic — A: hypersensitive. B: historically significant.
C: uncouth. D: excessively dramatic.

derisory — A: amusing. B: unfortunate. C: ridiculous.
D: damaging.

unprepossessing — A: poverty-stricken. B: unimpressive.
C: distinctive. D: laid-back.

condone — A: forgive. B: eliminate. C: regret. D: advise.

rail — A: rush through. B: punish. C: attack verbally.
D: lament.

66The difference between the impossible and the
possible lies in a person's determination.99

—TOMMY LASORDA

pallid — C: Lacking colour, vitality or interest; as, "He recalled Blaney's *pallid* and innocuous watercolours." Latin *pallidus*.

cumbersome — C: Unwieldy; as, "her *cumbersome* shoulder-bag flapping against her ribs." Old French *combrer* (to hinder).

raucous — C: Loud and harsh; rowdy; as, "the *raucous* beat of the music." Latin *raucus* (hoarse).

cursory — D: Superficial; hasty; as, "a *cursory* glance at the serial killer." Latin *currere* (to run).

clutch — A: A cluster, group or bunch; as, "a *clutch* of chief constables." Old Norse *klekja* (to hatch).

concomitant — B: Occurring together; accompanying; as, "Success has its *concomitant* disadvantages." Latin *concomitari* (to follow).

reticent — C: Reserved; not speaking openly or revealing one's thoughts. Latin *reticere* (to be silent).

condolences — B: Expressions of sympathy or comfort; as, "a formal visit of *condolence*." Latin *com-* (with) and *dolere* (to grieve).

ostensibly — D: Apparently but not necessarily so; as, *Ostensibly* he was there to teach. Latin *ostendere* (to show).

sobriquet — D: Nickname; an assumed, often humorous name; as, "a *sobriquet* both childish and basically unsuitable." French.

lugubrious — A: Mournful or sad, especially in an exaggerated way; as, "a look of *lugubrious* disapproval." Latin *lugere* (to bewail).

frisson — A: A shudder or shiver arising from fear, joy, excitement; as, "an agreeable *frisson* of terror." French.

venue — B: Meeting or gathering place. Also, location for a trial. French, from *venir* (to come).

recrimination — C: Countercharge; as, "Friendship there could deteriorate into gossip, *recriminations* and betrayal." Latin *re-* (again) and *criminari* (to accuse).

vicarious — D: Serving as a substitute; as, "a brief, *vicarious* immortality." Latin *vicarius*.

histrionic — D: Excessively dramatic; as, "He beat his hands against the door. It seemed a *histrionic* gesture." Latin *histrio* (actor).

derisory — C: Expressing mockery or contempt; ridiculous; as, "What you pay [in rent] is *derisory*. It doesn't even cover repairs." Latin *deridere* (to laugh).

unprepossessing — B: Unimpressive; not especially attractive; as, "a particularly *unprepossessing* face." Latin *in-* (not) and *possidere* (to possess).

condone — A: Forgive or overlook a wrongdoing; as, a man "who had never supposed that the evil of the world should be *condoned*." Latin *condonare*.

rail — C: Attack with harsh or insulting language; complain; as, "She *railed* at me like a woman possessed." Latin *ragere* (to bray).

Vocabulary Ratings

    9 — 11 correct . . . Good

    12 — 17 correct . . . Excellent

    18 — 20 correct . . . Exceptional

AND AWAY WE GO

Stalking through the cornfield . . . Blazing past the fire station . . . Slipping through the lingerie department . . .Tripping through the travel agency . . . Lumbering through the woods . . .

—DAVE AND EMILY NOSSAMAN

MUSIC TO THE EARS

The following words come from the witty musicals of Gilbert and Sullivan—The Mikado, The Pirates of Penzance, H.M.S. Pinafore *and others that have delighted millions. Choose the answer you think is correct. Turn the page for your score.*

mope — A: be dejected. B: wipe away. C: rebuff. D: mumble.

oration — A: speech. B: choral sound. C: ceremony. D: decoration.

quick — A: short ribbon. B: steep path. C: anything flimsy. D: deepest feelings.

dictatorial — A: clearly spoken. B: overbearing. C: repetitious. D: cranky.

paradox — A: parallel line. B: traditional belief. C: apparent contradiction. D: embarrassing muddle.

dissemble — A: disguise. B: take apart. C: scatter. D: fluster.

malediction — A: mispronunciation. B: soothing language. C: habit. D: curse.

bulwark — A: defence. B: firmness. C: compartment. D: platform.

solecism — A: wise saying. B: witty quip. C: clever argument. D: grammatical error.

succinct — A: sarcastic. B: outspoken. C: terse. D: slow and careful.

❝Laughter translates into any language.❞

—*"Graffiti," McNaught Syndicate*

reprobation — A: review. B: disapproval. C: endorsement.
    D: aversion.
bias — A: fairness. B: logical thought. C: prejudice.
    D: puzzling situation.
avidity — A: mental keenness. B: bitterness. C: thoughtless haste.
    D: intense desire.
suppliant — one who A: is a flatterer. B: has flexibility.
    C: fulfils a need. D: asks humbly.
propriety — A: truthfulness. B: punctuality. C: respectability.
    D: esteem.
atone — A: sing together. B: repent. C: adjust to. D: clarify.
induce — A: persuade. B: meet. C: accompany. D: decrease.
plaintiff — person who A: sues. B: is unhappy. C: defends.
    D: implores.
conundrum — A: joke. B: illustration. C: type of prayer.
    D: riddle.
unavailing — A: restrained. B: out of touch. C: useless.
    D: inevitable.

"The other arts persuade us, but music
takes us by surprise.**"**

—*EDUARD HANSLICK*

 ANSWERS

mope — A: Be dejected; gloomy; as, "I used to *mope* and sigh and pant, just like a lovesick boy." Middle Dutch *moppen* (to pout).

oration — A: Public speech, usually formal; as, "All thieves who could afford my fees relied on my *orations*." Latin *orare* (to speak).

quick — D: Deepest feelings; sensitive flesh under fingernails; as, "Your words cut me to the *quick*." Old English *cwicu* (living).

dictatorial — B: Overbearing; domineering; as, "His energetic fist should be ready to resist a *dictatorial* word." Latin *dictare* (to say often).

paradox — C: Apparent contradiction that may contain a truth; as, "We lay and sobbed upon the rocks, until to somebody occurred a startling *paradox*." Greek *paradoxos* (unbelievable).

dissemble — A: Disguise; hide one's identity; as, "Red, am I? and round—and rosy! Maybe, for I have *dissembled* well." Latin *dis-* (completely) and *simulare* (to pretend).

malediction — D: Curse; slander; as, "We'll finish his moral affliction by a very complete *malediction*." Latin *malus* (bad) and *dicere* (to speak).

bulwark — A: Defence; protection; as, "Never forget that they [sailors] are the *bulwarks* of England's greatness." Middle English *bulwerk*.

solecism — D: Grammatical error; as, "*solecisms* that society would never pardon." Greek *soloikos* (speaking incorrectly).

succinct — C: Terse; concise; as, "So, he decreed in words *succinct*, that all who flirted, leered or winked should be beheaded." Latin *succinctus*.

reprobation — B: Disapproval; scolding; as, "In uttering a *reprobation* to any British tar [sailor], I try to speak with moderation, but you have gone too far." Latin *reprobare* (to reject).

bias — C: Prejudice; inclination; as, "Free from *bias* of every kind, this trial must be tried." French *biais* (slant, slope).

avidity — D: Intense desire; greediness; as, "To dine on chops and roly-poly pudding with *avidity*." Latin *avere* (to crave).

suppliant — D: One who asks humbly; as, "Behold a *suppliant* at your feet." Latin *supplicare* (to beg).

propriety — C: Respectability; conformity; as, "*Propriety*, we know, says we ought to stay." Middle English *propriete*.

atone — B: Repent; make amends; as, "Oh, perjured lover, *atone, atone!*" Middle English *atonen* (to reconcile).

induce — A: Persuade, often subtly; as, "An official utterance might *induce* her to look upon your offer in its proper light." Latin *in-* (in) and *ducere* (to lead).

plaintiff — A: Person who sues; as, "Oh, listen to the *plaintiff*'s case." Old French *plaintif* (complaining).

conundrum — D: Riddle answered by a pun; as, "Good fellow in *conundrums* you are speaking . . . . The answer to them vainly I am seeking." Origin unknown.

unavailing — C: Useless; futile; as, "I thank you for your proffered solace, but it is *unavailing*." English *un-* (not) and Latin *valere* (to be strong).

Vocabulary Ratings
> 9 — 11 correct ... Good
> 12 — 17 correct ... Excellent
> 18 — 20 correct ... Exceptional

MUSICAL MIGHT-HAVE-BEENS

Bach "To the Future"

Handel "With Care"

Haydn "Seek"

Verdi "Interesting" —James M. Garber

MAGICAL MYSTERY

"There are two types of geniuses, the 'ordinary' and the 'magicians,'" says one admirer of Richard Feynman in a biography of the late physicist, who certainly belonged to the latter category. The following words are taken from the book. Turn the page to find your score.

rebuttal — A: suggestion. B: rebuke. C: unkind refusal.
D: opposing argument.

metamorphosis — A: deep sleep. B: transformation.
C: periodic recurrence. D: significant event.

cauldron — A: computer term. B: kettle. C: static electricity.
D: laser fusion.

esoteric — A: ancient. B: difficult to understand. C: wondrous.
D: light and frothy.

cadre — A: hidden source. B: follower. C: key group.
D: student.

rigour — A: anxiety. B: strictness. C: strength. D: vitality.

tenet — A: experiment. B: mathematical equation.
C: observation. D: belief or principle.

vantage — A: competitive superiority. B: pride. C: cutting edge.
D: turning point.

interpolate — A: clarify. B: investigate. C: reverse. D: insert.

superlative — A: supreme. B: powerful. C: legendary.
D: necessary.

❝We all live under the same sky, but we don't all have
the same horizon.**❞**

—KONRAD ADENAUER

rectify — A: break. B: correct. C: build. D: criticise.

truism — A: guess. B: questionable statement. C: discovery.
     D: obvious truth.

bailiwick — A: area of authority. B: woven container.
     C: false lead. D: complicated formula.

gestation — A: pregnancy. B: bodily motion. C: spurt of activity.
     D: period of quiet.

innate — A: resourceful. B: inborn. C: foolish. D: spontaneous.

subordinate — A: guide craftily. B: hand over. C: put under
     authority. D: add to.

embody — A: make similar. B: incorporate. C: separate.
     D: solidify.

connive — A: conspire. B: provoke. C: blame. D: tease.

primer — A: chemical symbol. B: introductory textbook.
     C: principal force. D: primitive drive.

teleological — related to the study of A: ultimate purposes.
     B: analytical procedures. C: communication.
     D: historic events.

" Never a daisy grows but a mystery guides the
growing. **"**

—RICHARD REALF

 ANSWERS

rebuttal — D: An opposing argument; as, "He offered the mildest of the many possible *rebuttals*." Old French *rebuter* (to thrust back, push).

metamorphosis — B: Transformation; complete change; as, the *metamorphosis* of a caterpillar into a butterfly. Greek *meta-morphoun* (to transform).

cauldron — B: Large kettle; also, an agitated condition; as, "the famous *caldron* of physicist Ernest Lawrence's laboratory." Latin *calidus* (warm).

esoteric — B: Difficult to understand; as, "Younger scientists explored *esoteric* new domains." Greek *esoteros* (inner).

cadre — C: Key group; nucleus of trained people; as, "He left behind a small *cadre* of students." Latin *quadrum* (square).

rigour — B: Strictness or severity in judgement or conduct; as, His childhood was a "combination of freedom and moral *rigour*." Latin *rigere* (to be stiff).

tenet — D: Belief or principle; as, "Only rarely did they express [their creed's] *tenets*, but they lived by them." Latin *tenere* (to hold).

vantage — A: Competitive superiority; position giving a broad perspective; as, the *vantage* that comes from experience. Old French *avantage*.

interpolate — D: Insert new material that may distort a text; mathematically, to estimate a missing value. Latin *interpolare* (to polish, corrupt).

superlative — A: Supreme; of outstanding quality. Latin *superlatus* (exaggerated).

rectify — B: Correct; adjust; amend; as, "to *rectify* his mother's cheque-book." Latin *rectificare*.

truism — D: Obvious, self-evident truth; as, "It became an instant *truism* that science meant power." Old English *treowth* (truth).

bailiwick — A: Area of authority, interest or skill; as, Quantum mechanics was his *bailiwick*. English *bailiff* (deputy sheriff) and *wick* (village).

gestation — A: Pregnancy. Also, the conception and development of an idea; as, the *gestation* of a new theory. Latin *gerere* (to bear).

innate — B: Inborn; existing naturally, rather than acquired; as, "Children are *innate* scientists." Latin *innasci*.

subordinate — C: Put under the authority of another; as, "Some [scientists] *subordinated* their own abilities to his." Latin *subordinare*.

embody — B: Incorporate; represent; give form to; as, "Most physicists were now persuaded that the atom *embodied* . . . electrons, protons and neutrons." Prefix *em-* (in) and *body*.

connive — A: Conspire; co-operate secretly; as, They *connived* to alert the president to the possibility of an atom bomb. Latin *connivere* (to close the eyes, wink).

primer — B: Introductory textbook covering the basic elements of a subject; as, a *primer* on mathematical methods. Latin *primus* (first).

teleological — A: Related to the study of ultimate purposes in natural phenomena; as, The *teleological* question, what is the meaning of life? Greek *telos* (end) and *-logy* (study of).

Vocabulary Ratings

     9 — 11 correct . . . Good
     12 — 17 correct . . . Excellent
     18 — 20 correct . . . Exceptional

"Everyone is a genius at least once a year.**"**

—*G. C. LICHTENBERG*

MUSIC OF POETRY

There's music in words, especially in the cadences of poetry, from which the verbs in this list come. Indicate your answer, then turn the page to rate your score.

vegetate — To A: be passive. B: be health conscious. C: eat no meat. D: rest.

sedate — To A: calm. B: give up. C: sit. D: keep under control.

stipulate — To A: undertake. B: be firm. C: specify. D: fasten tightly.

acclimatise — To A: moderate. B: acquire. C: reach a climax. D: adapt to.

berate — To A: underestimate. B: scold. C: make the cry of a donkey. D: classify.

relegate — To A: control by rules. B: act as a spokesman. C: put off or delay. D: send away.

equivocate — To A: stir up. B: be evasive. C: balance out. D: see all sides of a question.

renovate — To A: change. B: restore. C: replace. D: examine.

precipitate — To A: cause to happen. B: leap. C: clarify. D: make public.

exonerate — To A: become larger. B: free from blame. C: compliment excessively. D: destroy utterly.

WORD FOR WORD
Words are the clothes that thoughts wear.
—*Ronald Geller*
Metaphors are ideas sporting borrowed coats.
—*Emily Stronk*
Poetry is prose dressed in Sunday best.
—*O. C. M.*

innovate — To A: give courage to. B: study the cosmos.
C: re-establish. D: introduce something new.

extrapolate — To A: firm up. B: estimate. C: remove from. D: add to.

satiate — To A: desire. B: be cruel. C: use ridicule. D: glut.

recapitulate — To A: surrender. B: be indecisive. C: summarise.
D: retract.

undulate — To A: quiver and quake. B: move in waves.
C: revolve around. D: become seasick.

gesticulate — To A: frown. B: develop slowly.
C: make expressive gestures. D: pronounce distinctly.

immolate — To A: offer in sacrifice. B: keep from moving.
C: immerse completely. D: shield from.

militate — To A: challenge. B: lay down the law. C: arbitrate.
D: influence against.

crenellate — To A: wrinkle. B: notch. C: decorate with ribbons.
D: do brain studies.

perpetuate — A: to cause to continue. B: sulk. C: impose.
D: bring about.

66 In the end, the poem is not a thing we see; it is,

rather, a light by which we may see—and what

we see is life. **99**

—ROBERT PENN WARREN

vegetate — A: To live a life of passivity, monotony or mental inactivity; also, to grow as a plant. Latin *vegetare* (to quicken, enliven).

sedate — A: To calm or quiet by administering a drug; as, to *sedate* a ferocious animal in a zoo. Latin *sedare* (to settle).

stipulate — C: To specify as an essential condition of an agreement; as, He *stipulated* that the software program must be easy to learn. Latin *stipulari* (to bargain).

acclimatise — D: To adapt to new conditions or circumstances; as, to *acclimatise* to the slower pace of the tropics. French *acclimater*.

berate — B: To give a prolonged, severe and sometimes abusive scolding. English prefix *be-* (thoroughly) and *rate* (to chide).

relegate — D: To send away, especially to a less desirable situation. Also, to delegate; as, to *relegate* a problem to a committee. Latin *relegare*.

equivocate — B: To be evasive, vague or ambiguous so as to mislead or conceal; hedge. Latin *aequus* (equal) and *vocare* (to call).

renovate — B: To restore to a good condition; as, The family *renovated* an old house. Latin *renovare*.

precipitate — A: To cause to happen suddenly; bring on; as, His unfortunate remark *precipitated* a bitter argument. Latin *praecipitare* (to hurl downward).

exonerate — B: To free or clear from blame; absolve; as, to *exonerate* an accused person on the basis of fresh evidence. Latin *ex-* (out) and *onus* (burden).

innovate — D: To introduce something new or create a novel method of doing something. Latin *in-* (in) and *novare* (to make new).

extrapolate — B: To estimate; also, to draw a conclusion about something unknown based on its relevance to known facts; as, to *extrapolate* a theory about a tenth planet. Latin *extra-* (beyond) and *polire* (to polish).

satiate — D: To glut; have more than enough of anything to the point of losing interest; as, to *satiate* oneself with cheesecake. Latin *satiare* (to satisfy, fill).

recapitulate — C: To summarise concisely, as at the end of a speech or meeting; review briefly. Latin *recapitulare*.

undulate — B: To move in a smooth, wave-like or sinuous motion; as, fields of wheat *undulating* in the soft wind. Latin *unda* (wave).

gesticulate — C: To make expressive gestures with the hands and arms to add emphasis to one's words. Latin *gesticulari*.

immolate — A: To offer in sacrifice; to kill as by fire; as, The Buddhist monk, opposing the government, *immolated* himself in a bonfire. Latin *immolare* (originally, to sprinkle with sacrificial meal).

militate — D: To have a substantial influence or effect, usually against; as, The policy will *militate* against age discrimination. Latin *militare* (to serve as a soldier).

crenellate — B: To form square notches in moulding; make squared-off battlements in a fortress. Old French *crénel* (notch).

perpetuate — A: To cause to continue or be remembered; as, to *perpetuate* a tradition. Latin *perpetuare*.

Vocabulary Ratings
> 9 — 11 correct . . . Good
> 12 — 17 correct . . . Excellent
> 18 — 20 correct . . . Exceptional

"It's a little bit the fiddle, but lots more who holds the bow.**"**

—*WILBURN WILSON*

IN TWAIN ENGLISH

Besides being a writer, Mark Twain was also an inventor, a river pilot, a humorist and a lecturer. How many of the following words, all taken from his books, do you know? Turn the page to find out.

insipid — A: not interesting. B: slow-moving. C: lacking in thoroughness. D: easy-going.

sovereign — A: entirety. B: wealth. C: ruler. D: grandeur.

singularly — A: simply. B: extraordinarily. C: representatively. D: pointedly.

inundation — A: a sinking. B: repetition. C: flood. D: curve.

husband — A: conserve. B: boss around. C: be fond of. D: relieve.

rude — A: projecting. B: natural. C: everyday. D: primitive.

trammels — A: problems. B: blows or punches. C: narrow planks. D: restraints.

yaw — A: open wide. B: change direction. C: tell tall tales. D: scold.

unfettered — A: slim. B: without principle. C: liberated. D: careless.

somnambulist — A: magician. B: sleepwalker. C: acrobat. D: wine steward.

sound — A: leave suddenly. B: proceed. C: play the fool. D: measure water depth.

❝Whenever you find yourself on the side of the majority, it is time to pause and reflect.**❞**

—MARK TWAIN

---

remonstrate — A: feel regret. B: be angry. C: argue in protest.
D: have sympathy for.

farce — A: social blunder. B: absurd sham. C: disorder.
D: falsehood.

pretext — A: false reason. B: first draft. C: introduction.
D: summary.

lagniappe — A: compliment. B: lasso. C: mugginess.
D: small gift.

hobnob — A: scold. B: flirt. C: associate with. D: snub.

finite — A: complete. B: limited. C: exact. D: everlasting.

bogus — A: inferior. B: spooky. C: not genuine. D: extra.

elision — A: home of the gods. B: injury or wound.
C: omission of a syllable. D: careful explanation.

misnomer — A: wrong name. B: sales pitch. C: random list.
D: gross insult.

" There ain't no surer way to find out whether you like people or hate them than to travel with them. **"**

—MARK TWAIN

 *ANSWERS*

insipid — A: Not interesting; without flavour; as, "the *insipid* diversion they call croquet." Latin *in-* (not) and *sapidus* (savoury).

sovereign — C: Ruler; monarch; king; supreme authority. Old French *souverain*.

singularly — B: Extraordinarily; exceptionally; as, "So *singularly* clear was the water, the boat seemed to be floating in air." Latin *singularis* (single).

inundation — C: Flood; overwhelming flow; as, "A Mississippi River *inundation* is the next most wasting infliction to a fire." Latin *inundare* (to overflow).

husband — A: Conserve; use economically; make the most of. Old English *husbonda* (master of the house).

rude — D: Primitive; crude; roughly made; as, "They found some *rude* and fantastic Indian paintings." Latin *rudis*.

trammels — D: Restraints; whatever hinders free action; as, "The watchman threw off all *trammels* of date and locality." Middle English *tramaile* (fishing net).

yaw — B: Change direction in a boat or ship; swerve from side to side; as, "I *yawed* too far from shore." Origin uncertain.

unfettered — C: Liberated; free from restriction; as, "A river pilot was the only *unfettered* and entirely independent human being." English *un* (not) and Old English *feter* (chain or shackle).

somnambulist — B: Sleepwalker; as, He was a *somnambulist* who once steered a difficult passage in his sleep. Latin *somnus* (sleep) and *ambulare* (to walk).

sound — D: Measure the depth of water with a weighted line; as, The words "mark twain" mean the bottom has been *sounded* at two fathoms (12 feet). Latin *subundare* (to submerge).

remonstrate — C: Argue in protest; as, "I *remonstrated* with him about [whistling at the funeral]." Latin *remonstrare* (to demonstrate).

farce — B: Absurd sham; as, "those sorrowful *farces* we call a jury trial." Latin *farcire* (to stuff).

pretext — A: False reason to cover up the real one; excuse; as, looking for a *pretext* to find fault. Latin *praetexere* (to pretend).

lagniappe — D: Small gift, especially to a customer; as, "We picked up a word worth travelling to New Orleans to get; a nice, limbre, expressive, handy word — *lagniappe*." Creole, from American Spanish *lañapa*.

hobnob — C: Associate with; as, "to *hobnob* with nobility." Originally a reference to drinking together. From Old English *habben* (to have) and *nabban* (not to have).

finite — B: Limited; having boundaries; as, a *finite* number of hours in a day. Latin *finire* (to finish).

bogus — C: Not genuine; counterfeit; as, "Nobody had ever received his *bogus* history as gospel before." Origin uncertain.

elision — C: Omission of a syllable, such as "o'er" for "over"; as, "I found the half-forgotten Southern *elisions* pleasing to my ear." Latin *elidere* (to strike out).

misnomer — A: Wrong or unsuitable name; as, "'The Grand Holy Land Pleasure Excursion' was a *misnomer*." Old French *mesnommer* (to misname).

Vocabulary Ratings
> 9 — 11 correct . . . Good
> 12 — 17 correct . . . Excellent
> 18 — 20 correct . . . Exceptional

SNIDELINERS

She's so aggravating, she'd give an aspirin a headache.

—Frank Hughes

He'd toss a drowning man both ends of a rope. —Michael R. Luna

He's so snobbish, he won't even ride in the same car as his chauffeur. —David Frost

CRITICAL JUDGEMENTS

Thumbs-up ratings by reviewers can often determine the success of a television programme, book, recording or movie. What are your "critic's choice" definitions of the following words picked from reviews of the arts? Turn the page for your score.

blathering — A: foolish-talking. B: crying. C: gossiping.
D: outrageous.

buoyant — A: shallow. B: amusing. C: lighthearted. D: brisk.

static — A: muddled. B: bunched up. C: tedious. D: stationary.

rue — A: scold. B: be unsympathetic. C: designate.
D: regret.

evocative — A: challenging. B: stimulating memories. C: loud.
D: speaking clearly.

gull — A: soothe. B: soar. C: deceive. D: irritate.

execrable — A: detestable. B: harsh. C: flawless.
D: extraordinary.

muse — A: fuss over. B: mumble. C: yearn deeply. D: ponder.

brio — A: danger. B: vivacity. C: informality. D: sluggishness.

deracinate — A: distribute. B: explain carefully. C: solve logically.
D: uproot.

imprecation — A: belief. B: warning. C: curse. D: blessing.

SO AND SO'S

He's so crooked he could hide behind a corkscrew. —Lane Kirkland

He's so tough he looks as if he flosses with piano wire.

—Christopher Buckley

Coffee so strong it would keep you up three days
after you died. —Marv Albert

CRITICS' CORNER

pedestrian — A: long-term. B: dull. C: healthy. D: dependable.

trilogy — A: set of three. B: musical scale. C: medical priority.
D: long story.

specious — A: genuine. B: roomy. C: misleading. D: dreamy.

contrive — A: to strive after. B: work together. C: think up.
D: tempt.

cameo — A: minor role for actor. B: something added.
C: old-fashioned plot. D: style or manner.

audacious — A: conceited. B: loud. C: full of energy.
D: recklessly bold.

sycophantic — A: cowardly. B: flattering. C: highly intelligent.
D: rhythmic.

prolific — A: skilful. B: wordy. C: productive. D: proud.

stilted — A: stiff. B: forceful. C: carefully worked out.
D: repressed.

PAN ALLEY

From a review: "Television is so dull this season that children
are doing their homework."

—PEMBROKE, MASS., SILVER LAKE NEWS

Comment on a show touted as light and breezy: "I was
expecting fluff, but this was lint."

—CAROLYN FORD

 ANSWERS

blathering — A: Talking in a foolish way and usually at length; as, These characters are *blathering* idiots. Old Norse *blathr* (nonsense).

buoyant — C: Showing a light-hearted resilience of spirit; as, She bubbles with *buoyant* energy. Also, able to float. Perhaps Spanish *boyar* (to float).

static — D: Stationary; not moving; inactive; as, The actor's performance was *static* and lifeless. Greek *statikos* (causing to stand).

rue — D: Regret a mistake; feel remorse or repentance; as, He *rued* his decision to direct the controversial film. Old English *hreowan* (to regret).

evocative — B: Stimulating a memory, mood or mental image; as, The country-western singer's ballads are magically *evocative*. Latin *evocare* (to call out).

gull — C: Deceive or cheat; as, She was *gulled* into going off with the con man. Origin uncertain.

execrable — A: Detestable; abominable; very bad; as, He writes *execrable* fiction. Latin *exsecrari* (to curse).

muse — D: Ponder; consider thoughtfully; meditate; as, "It's more than an action story," the reviewer *mused*.
Old French *muser*.

brio — B: Vivacity; liveliness; dash and spirit; as, The play has a lot of *brio* and a few bumps. Italian, from Celtic *brigos*.

deracinate — D: Uproot; eradicate; remove from a natural environment; as, to describe the pain of being *deracinated* from one's native land. French *de-* (out) and *racine* (root).

imprecation — C: Vengeful curse or wish that calls for a calamity to fall on someone; as, a man of muttered *imprecations* and brooding silences. Latin *imprecari* (to invoke evil on).

pedestrian — B: Dull and ordinary; without vitality, imagination or distinction; as, a *pedestrian* film. Latin *pedester* (on foot).

trilogy — A: Set of three related works; as, the second novel of the *trilogy*. Greek *tri-* (three) and *logos* (word).

specious — C: Misleading; seeming to be true but actually false; as, The rumour raised its *specious* head again. Latin *speciosus* (beautiful, plausible).

contrive — C: Think up; plan cleverly; conspire; as, The scenes were the most bizarre that the director could *contrive*. Old French *controver*.

cameo — A: Minor role for an actor, especially a famous one; short piece of descriptive writing. Primary meaning is engraved gem Italian *cammeo*.

audacious — D: Recklessly bold; highly original and inventive; uninhibited; as, The director's imagery has always been *audacious*. Latin *audere* (to dare).

sycophantic — B: Flattering in a self-seeking, servile way; as, The movie star's biography is a glossy, *sycophantic* portrait. Greek *sykophantes* (informer).

prolific — C: Highly productive; turning out many creative works; fertile; as, She is a *prolific* writer. Latin *proles* (offspring).

stilted — A: Stiff; artificially formal; pompous; without a sense of grace and flow; as, a play with *stilted* situations and dialogue.

Vocabulary Ratings
- 9 — 11 correct . . . Good
- 12 — 17 correct . . . Excellent
- 18 — 20 correct . . . Exceptional

VOCAL CHORDS
He had a voice so husky it could pull a dog sled.
—RAYMOND TILLMANN

KEYS TO LEARNING

Keeping your spoken and written language fresh takes constant effort, learning new words day by day. In this quiz, choose the word or phrase that best defines the key word. Turn the page to check your score. Try to add any missed words to your permanent collection.

tender — A: offer. B: sympathise. C: hesitate. D: suggest.

ardour — A: persuasion. B: warmth of emotion. C: deep conviction. D: musical inclination.

clinical — A: abstract. B: cosmetic. C: directly observed. D: drug-induced.

sufferance — A: right to vote. B: inner peace. C: give-and-take situation. D: patient endurance.

boisterous — A: humorously pompous. B: carefree and nonchalant. C: noisy and cheerful. D: invigorating.

factoid — A: splinter group. B: obvious mistake. C: unverified information. D: synthetic object.

beggar — A: explain. B: make seem inadequate. C: attempt to deceive. D: impose limitations.

conversant — A: talkative. B: courteous. C: well-informed. D: creative.

icon — A: symbol. B: false representation. C: document. D: destroyer of images.

obstinate — A: protruding. B: unyielding. C: foolish. D: self-assertive.

❝You will stay young as long as you learn, form new habits and don't mind being contradicted.**❞**

—Marie von Ebner-Eschenbach

---

spontaneous — A: well-timed. B: comical. C: explosive.
 D: unplanned.
fraught — A: full of. B: manufactured. C: empty. D: bitter.
cashier — A: assist. B: save. C: win. D: dismiss.
prophetic — A: scolding. B: predictive. C: obscure. D: ancient.
sundry — A: countless. B: changing. C: various. D: disconnected.
implication — something A: proven. B: cursed. C: causing doubt.
 D: hinted at.
endeavour — A: look over. B: please. C: attempt. D: bring about.
impoverished — A: imposed upon. B: severely penalised.
 C: made poor. D: heavily burdened.
pithiness — A: ridicule. B: indecency. C: conciseness.
 D: determination.
tremulous — A: delicate. B: tranquil. C: inadequate.
 D: quivering.

tender — A: Offer or present anything for acceptance or approval; as, The administration expected the official to *tender* his resignation. Latin *tendere* (to extend).

ardour — B: Intense warmth of emotion; zeal; as, The student spoke with *ardour* of the need to improve the educational system. Latin *ardor* (flame).

clinical — C: Relating to the direct observation and treatment of patients; as, *Clinical* tests showed him to be in good health. Greek *klinikos* (of the bed).

sufferance — D: Patient endurance; capacity to tolerate pain or distress; as, She bore the harsh winters with stoic *sufferance*. Latin *sufferre* (to undergo).

boisterous — C: Noisy and cheerful; rowdy and unrestrained; as, The grandfather gave a *boisterous* laugh. Middle English *boistreous* (crude).

factoid — C: Unverified or fictitious information presented as fact; as, a report filled with *factoids*. Also, obscure, trivial information. From *fact* and Greek *-oid* (resembling).

beggar — B: Make descriptions or comparisons seem inadequate or useless; outdo; as, a spectacular scene that *beggars* description. Middle English *beggere* (to make poor).

conversant — C: Well-informed; familiar with; as, a sales manager *conversant* with a competitor's marketing plan. Latin *conversari* (to keep company with).

icon — A: Symbol; image; representation; as, Unfortunately, sometimes a mansion becomes the main *icon* of worldly success. Greek *eikon* (image).

obstinate — B: Unyielding; unreasonably resolved to have one's way; stubborn; as, We call someone "persevering" in a good cause and *"obstinate"* in a bad one. Latin *obstinare* (to persist).

spontaneous — D: Unplanned; coming naturally and freely on its own; as, the audience's *spontaneous* applause. Latin *sponte* (of its own accord).

fraught — A: Full of; involving; laden; as, The government's plan was *fraught* with difficulties. Middle Dutch *vrachten* (to load a ship).

cashier — D: Dismiss from a position of authority or trust, especially in disgrace; as, The lieutenant was *cashiered* from his regiment. Old French *casser* (to annul).

prophetic — B: Predictive, often ominously so; foreshadowing. Greek *prophetikos*.

sundry — C: Various; miscellaneous; as, *sundry* household tasks. Old English *syndrig* (separate).

implication — D: Something hinted at but not expressed in overt terms; as, the *implication* that the bookkeeper was involved in the fraud. Latin *implicare* (to enfold).

endeavour — C: Make an attempt; strive; as, The United Nations *endeavours* to bring peace to the region. Old French *deveir* (duty).

impoverished — C: Made poor; as, an *impoverished* nation. Also, without strength or richness; as, an *impoverished* vocabulary. From *in* and Latin *pauper* (poor).

pithiness — C: Conciseness; fullness of meaning with brevity of expression; as, The minister had the gift of *pithiness*. Old English *pith* (kernel, pit of a fruit).

tremulous — D: Quivering from nervousness, grief, weakness or fear; as, The survivor spoke in a *tremulous* voice. Latin *tremere* (to tremble).

Vocabulary Ratings

        9 — 11 correct ... Good
      12 — 17 correct ... Excellent
      18 — 20 correct ... Exceptional

ONWARDS AND UPWARDS

Each of the following words is tougher than the one before it—until the final few, which can stump even those with the strongest vocabularies. Climb this mountain of useful words and you'll reach new vistas of understanding. Then turn the page to check your elevation.

jeopardy — A: venture. B: gamble. C: danger. D: challenge.

guerrilla — A: jungle animal. B: fighter. C: daredevil. D: cheat.

escapade — A: close call. B: surprise gift. C: long journey. D: reckless adventure.

dynasty — A: historical fiction. B: hereditary rulers. C: political junta. D: interim government.

influx — A: pulsating sound. B: removal. C: absorption. D: inflow.

euphoria — A: eccentricity. B: love. C: mystical experience. D: elation.

decor — A: decoration. B: manners. C: neckline. D: braid.

inertia — A: exhaustion. B: powerful force. C: sluggishness. D: stubbornness.

binary — made up of: A: various connections. B: two parts. C: building materials. D: unlike elements.

entente — A: difficulty. B: celebration. C: friendly understanding. D: secret meeting.

66Let me tell you the secret that has led me to my goal. My strength lies solely in my tenacity.99

—LOUIS PASTEUR

"No one can arrive from being talented alone. God gives talent; work transforms talent into genius."

—ANNA PAVLOVA, *QUOTED IN* LOS ANGELES EXAMINER

inpunity — A: exemption from penalty. B: great honesty. C: bitter criticism. D: blind self-confidence.

earthy — A: creative. B: varied. C: uninhibited. D: heavy.

affluent — A: important. B: agreeable. C: rich. D: poised.

omnipotent — A: all-powerful. B: widespread. C: haughty. D: one-sided.

incursion — A: interruption. B: raid. C: insult. D: obstacle.

guileless — A: wishy-washy. B: modest. C: straightforward. D: easy-going.

panacea — A: turmoil. B: over-all view. C: cure-all. D: source of problems.

empirical — A: arrogant and demanding. B: based on experience. C: having delusions of grandeur. D: theoretical.

holograph — A: assumed name. B: compact disc. C: constellation. D: hand-written document.

gnomic — A: puzzling. B: shrunken. C: very humorous. D: wise and pithy.

"A life of ease is a difficult pursuit."

—WILLIAM COWPER

jeopardy — C: Danger; risk of loss; as, Accused of falsifying his research data, the scientist found his reputation in *jeopardy*. Old French *jeu parti* (divided game with even chances).

guerrilla — B: Fighter, especially an irregular soldier who uses hit-and-run tactics. Spanish (little war).

escapade — D: Reckless adventure or prank; as, a schoolyard *escapade*. Spanish *escapar* (to escape; flee).

dynasty — B: Hereditary line of rulers; series of family members noted for wealth or success; as the Rothschild *dynasty*. Greek *dynasthai* (to have power).

influx — D: Inflow; inpouring; as, Mexico's *influx* of tourists. Latin *influere*.

euphoria — D: Elation; sense of well-being. Greek *eu-* (well) and *pherein* (to bear).

decor — A: Decoration; style of furnishings, colours and the like in a home or office. French, from Latin *decor* (beauty).

inertia — C: Sluggishness; slowness to take action; as a nation paralysed by *inertia*. Latin, from *iners* (inactive).

binary — B: Made up of two parts: as, The analogue computer is based on a *binary* system of the digits 0 and 1. Latin *bini* (two by two).

entente — C: Friendly understanding between two, or among several, nations; as, U.S.-Canadian *entente* concerning their unfortified boundary. French, from *entendre* (to understand).

inpunity — A: Exemption from penalty or harmful consequences; as, He lied with *impunity*. Latin *in-* (without) and *poena* (punishment).

earthy — C: Uninhibited; natural; hearty; as, The public loved her *earthy* humour. Also, coarse, vulgar. Old English *eorthe* (earth).

affluent — C: Rich; prosperous; as, Japan has become an *affluent* society. Latin *affluere* (to flow to).

omnipotent — A: All-powerful; as, He suffered from the delusion that he was *omnipotent.* Latin *omnis* (all) and *potens* (able).

incursion — B: Sudden raid or invasion into another's territory; as, a terrorist *incursion* into Israel. Latin *incurrere* (to attack).

guileless — C: Straightforward; sincere; as, a *guileless* child. From English *guile* (slyness, cunning) and *-less* (without).

panacea — C: Cure-all for diseases or problems; as, There is no *panacea* for the world's economic ills. Greek *pan-* (all) and *akos* (healing).

empirical — B: Based on experience and observation rather than on theory; as, The *empirical* evidence was overwhelming. Greek *-en* (in) and *peira* (trial).

holograph — D: A document wholly written by hand by the person named as the author; as, a *holograph* will. From Greek *holographos.*

gnomic — D: Wise and pithy; as, The preacher was famous for his *gnomic* statements. Greek *gnome* (thought, judgement).

Vocabulary Ratings

    9 — 11 correct ... Good

    12 — 17 correct ... Excellent

    18 — 20 correct ... Exceptional

❝Even a sheet of paper is lighter when two people lift it.**❞**

—KOREAN PROVERB

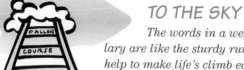

TO THE SKY

The words in a well-developed vocabulary are like the sturdy rungs in a ladder that help to make life's climb easier, as well as more pleasurable and successful. Take this quiz to check your progress; then turn the page for the correct answers.

concession — A: admission. B: courtesy. C: head injury.
   D: addition.

pallor — A: paleness. B: inflammation. C: paralysis. D: stretcher.

quagmire — A: quarry. B: pitfall. C: marsh. D: subatomic
   particle.

plangent — A: overripe. B: flat. C: loud and reverberating.
   D: robust.

demographics — A: governmental procedures. B: process of
   decoding. C: visual demonstration. D: population statistics.

vex — A: fuss. B: annoy. C: bewitch. D: shame.

legerdemain — A: sleight of hand. B: nonsense.
   C: act of postponing. D: storytelling.

palpably — A: throbbingly. B: carefully. C: obviously.
   D: sentimentally.

course — A: ruffle. B: plan. C: denounce. D: flow.

buttress — A: accessory. B: support. C: tower. D: busybody.

canvass — A: spread out. B: ask for opinions. C: criticise.
   D: cover up.

66Life begins as a quest of the child for the man and
ends as a journey by the man to rediscover the child.**99**

—LAURENS VAN DER POST, THE LOST WORLD OF THE KALAHARI (MORROW)

> **66**History celebrates few persons who waited
> for inspiration.**99**
>
> —*NED ARTHUR*

---

gamy — A: dashing. B: risky. C: plucky. D: sportsmanlike.

chapfallen — A: angry. B: rejected. C: untidy. D: dejected.

hacienda — A: grape arbour. B: after-meal nap. C: ranch.
D: porch.

in concert — A: sympathetically. B: together. C: apart.
D: publicly.

moribund — A: coming to an end. B: deferring or delaying.
C: binding securely. D: witty in a mean way.

onerous — A: threatening. B: immense. C: bad-smelling.
D: burdensome.

rationalise — A: parcel out. B: explain in minute detail.
C: justify. D: be optimistic.

philippic — A: humorous remark. B: bitter verbal denunciation.
C: wise saying. D: ironic observation.

synonymous — A: alike. B: boring. C: unknown. D: unvarying.

NIGHT LINES
The sky pulled a dark sheet over us and pinned it with stars.
—*BRYCE COURTENAY*

ANSWERS

concession — A: Admission, compromise, acknowledgment; as, mutual *concessions* of management and labour. Latin *concedere* (to yield).

pallor — A: Unusual paleness from ill health, fear, shock; as, the *pallor* of someone with heat stroke. Latin.

quagmire — C: Marsh; wet, soft ground; extremely difficult situation to get out of; as, a financial *quagmire*. English *quag* (bog) and *mire* (soggy ground).

plangent — C: Beating with a loud, deep, reverberating sound that rises and falls like breaking waves; as, *plangent* music for soap operas. Latin *plangere* (to beat).

demographics — D: Population statistics, such as income, purchasing habits, age; as, *Demographics* showed that the area could not support a new restaurant. Greek *demos* (people) and *graphein* (to write).

vex — B: Annoy, irritate, worry; as, to *vex* someone by being habitually late. Latin *vexare*.

legerdemain — A: Sleight of hand, as in performing magic; craftiness or trickery; as, the deft *legerdemain* of a sales pitch. French *léger de main* (light of hand).

palpably — C: Obviously; detectably; plainly; as, The actress plays a *palpably* lonely character. Latin *palpare* (to touch soothingly).

course — D: Flow or move swiftly; as, Before them *coursed* a wide river. Latin *currere* (to run).

buttress — B: Support or reinforcement; as, the stone *buttress* of a medieval cathedral, or the *buttress* of a parent's love. Old French *bouteret* (thrusting arch).

canvass — B: Ask for opinions, votes, orders; as, The reporter *canvassed* the neighbourhood's residents for stories. Origin uncertain.

gamy — C: Plucky, spirited; as, a *gamy* colt. Also, slightly tainted; as, *gamy* meat. English *game*.

chapfallen — D: Dejected; downhearted; as, She was *chapfallen* at not being promoted. Literally "having the lower jaw hanging down." From English *chop* (jaw) and *fallen*.

hacienda — C: Ranch or large estate in Spain or South America. Spanish, from Latin *facienda* (things to be done or made).

in concert — B: Together; in unison, agreement or harmony; as, The Czech people acted *in concert* for political reform. Italian *concertare* (to harmonize).

moribund — A: Coming to an end; dying; outdated; as, the *moribund* policies of some nations. Latin *mori* (to die).

onerous — D: Burdensome, laborious, troublesome; as, Some writers find proofreading manuscripts an *onerous* chore. Latin *onus* (load).

rationalise — C: Justify questionable actions with plausible but untrue reasons; as, An embezzler may *rationalise* that the company doesn't need the money he steals. Latin *rationalis* (reasonable).

philippic — B: Bitter verbal denunciation or attack; as, the Colombian president's brave *philippic* against the drug cartels. Greek, from Demosthenes' speeches against King Philip of Macedon.

synonymous — A: Alike; being a synonym of; equivalent in meaning. Greek *syn-* (together) and *onyma* (name).

Vocabulary Ratings
    9 — 11 correct . . . Good
    12 — 17 correct . . . Excellent
    18 — 20 correct . . . Exceptional

SKY LARKS
The clouds are playing charades.
—*JOSH CARDEN*

REPRISE

CATCHING WORDS

Paying attention is always important, but especially when facing the unfamiliar. Pay attention to the unfamiliar words in this quiz. Then turn the page to check your score.

garrison — A: military post. B: horse stable.
C: execution by choking. D: square tower.

inadmissible — A: unbelievable. B: false. C: unacceptable.
D: inarticulate.

reprise — A: vengeance. B: repetition. C: breathing spell.
D: cancellation.

deputation — A: expulsion from a country. B: delegation.
C: formal argument. D: statement made under oath.

irresolute — A: indecisive. B: careless. C: fully determined.
D: scattered.

provocateur — A: agitator. B: competitor. C: negotiator.
D: philosopher.

autocrat — A: member of the nobility. B: someone with absolute
power. C: instructor. D: patron.

luminary — A: floodlight. B: peaceful scene. C: celebrity.
D: clairvoyant person.

determinate — A: goal-oriented. B: vague. C: crucial.
D: distinct.

intuit — A: theorise. B: suggest. C: go into a trance.
D: know by hunch.

❝An error doesn't become a mistake until you
refuse to correct it.**❞**

—O. A. BATTISTA

66God made time, but man made haste.**99**
—IRISH PROVERB

veracity — A: speed. B: anger. C: energy. D: truthfulness.

cavalcade — A: waterfall. B: procession. C: avalanche.
D: sumptuous banquet.

martial — characteristic of A: war. B: marriage.
C: a large group. D: a wetland.

encode — A: transmit. B: pull back. C: put into cipher.
D: intercept.

ignoble— A: foolish. B: dishonourable. C: laughable. D: proud.

inception — A: idea. B: interruption. C: beginning.
D: social function.

implausible — A: inflexible. B: slipshod. C: unflappable.
D: unlikely.

addendum — A: something added. B: calculator.
C: order of business. D: large drum.

reticular — A: angular. B: circular. C: bowl-shaped. D: net-like.

felicitous — A: sentimental. B: appropriate. C: lucky.
D: scatterbrained.

MIXED MAXIMS
Don't count your chickens before they cross the road.
Mind your own business before pleasure.
He who laughs first shall be last.
Beauty is only skin deep in the eye of the beholder.
—DIANE CROSBY IN JEFF DAVIS COUNTY, GA., LEDGER

ANSWERS

garrison — A: Military post; troops stationed in a fortified place; as, a *garrison* at the edge of the frontier. Old French *garnison*.

inadmissible — C: Unacceptable; not allowable; as, The judge ruled the evidence to be *inadmissible*. Latin *in-* (not) and *admittere* (to admit).

reprise — B: Repetition of a passage of music; as, Gershwin's *reprise* of his major theme in "An American in Paris." Old French *reprendre* (to take back).

deputation — B: Delegation; group appointed to represent others; as, The *deputation* called on the mayor. Latin *deputare* (to assign).

irresolute — A: Indecisive; hesitating; uncertain about a course of action; as, His *irresolute* nature made him a poor executive. Latin *irresolutus*.

provocateur — A: Agitator; person who provokes trouble; as, The secret police placed *provocateurs* among the dissenters. Often designated *agent provocateur*. French.

autocrat — B: Someone with unlimited power over others; as, Today few successful corporations allow an *autocrat* to preside. Greek *autokrates* (ruling by oneself).

luminary — C: Celebrity; one who enlightens or influences others; as, Many *luminaries* gathered for the movie première. Latin *lumen* (light).

determinate — D: Distinct; having precisely defined limits; as, the *determinate* wording of a local building code. Latin *determinare* (to fix the limits of).

intuit — D: Know or learn by hunch; as, From her conversation he *intuited* a sensitive mind, serious and full of goodness. Latin *intueri* (to look at).

veracity — D: Truthfulness; honesty; accuracy; as, stories based more on humour than *veracity*. Latin *verus* (true).

cavalcade — B: Procession, especially of horseback riders or carriages; any series or sequence; as, Irving Berlin's *cavalcade* of hit songs. Latin *caballus* (horse).

martial — A: Characteristic of war or military life; as, *martial* music or a city under *martial* law. Latin, from *Mars* (Roman god of war).

encode — C: Put into cipher, a system of secret symbols. Latin *en-* (in) and *codex* (writing tablet).

ignoble — B: Dishonourable; mean-spirited; not noble in character or quality; as, So many of Stalin's *ignoble* actions stain the tapestry of history. Latin *ignobilis*.

inception — C: The beginning or start of something; as, The bride's aunt witnessed the *inception* of the couple's romance. Latin *incipere* (to begin).

implausible — D: Unlikely; difficult to believe; as, The student's elaborate excuse for being late sounded *implausible*. Latin *in-* (not) and *plaudere* (to applaud).

addendum — A: Something added; a supplement; as, The report had an *addendum* clarifying certain points. Latin *addere* (to add).

reticular — D: Net-like; intricate; tending to entangle; as, The lattice-work windows cast *reticular* shadows on the floor. Latin *reticulum* (little net).

felicitous — B: Appropriate; apt; well-suited for the occasion; as, The negotiator's *felicitous* anecdote broke the tension. Latin *felicitas* (happiness).

Vocabulary Ratings
>   9 — 11 correct . . . Good
>   12 — 17 correct . . . Excellent
>   18 — 20 correct . . . Exceptional

EVER NOTICE . . .
. . . that too many people don't know what's cooking until it boils over? —Arnold H. Glasow

TEXT CREDITS

This page constitutes a continuation of the copyright page at the front of the book.

19, Ludcke: Reprinted by permission of Cartoon Features Syndicate. **21**, Fellini: Copyright © 1993 by The New York Times Company. Reprinted by permission. **24**, Edwards: reprinted with permission of Time, Inc. **25**, Bradley: from *Black Trillium* by Marion Zimmer Bradley. Copyright © 1990 by Marion Zimmer Bradley, Julian May and Andre Norten. Reprinted by permission of Doubleday, a division of Bantam Doubleday Dell Publishing Group, Inc.; Ackerman: Copyright © 1990 by Diane Ackerman. Reprinted by permission of Random House, Inc.; Doug Larson reprinted by permission of United Feature Syndicate, Inc. **29**, Sarnoff: Copyright © 1973, Forbes, Inc. Reprinted by permission. **41**, Fosdick: Copyright 1941 by Harper & Brothers. Copyright renewed © 1968 by Harry Emerson Fosdick. Reprinted by permission of HarperCollins Publishers, Inc. **44**, Lippmann: used with permission of the President and Fellows of Harvard College. **49**, © Bernie Ward. **64**, "Optimists" © Copyrighted Chicago Tribune Company. All rights reserved. Used with permission. Tabak: reprinted by permission of Cartoon Features Syndicate. **65**, Dickson: Paul Dickson © 1981, reprinted by permission of the Helen Brann Agency. **69**, Michener: Copyright © 1982 by James A. Michener. Reprinted by permission of Random House, Inc. **71**, Reprinted by permission of Robert Orben. **75**, Copyright © 1970 Irene Alice Murdoch. Used by permission of Viking Penguin, a division of Penguin Books USA, Inc. **76**, Mistral: © 1922 (Spanish Institute of the United States). **77**, Weintraub: reprinted with permission, *Chicago Sun-Times* © 1995. **84**, Doug Larson reprinted by permission of United Feature Syndicate, Inc. **92**, Ashe: Copyright © 1993 by Arthur Ashe and Arnold Rampersad; Reprinted by permission of Alfred A. Knopf, Inc. **95**, Stanley: reprinted by permission of the *Columbus Journal-Republican.* **97**, © Catholic New York, 1994. **101**, reprinted by permission of Jude Wanniski. **103**, reprinted by permission of G. P. Putnam's Sons. **105**, Hamill: Copyright © 1988, reprinted by permission of *Esquire*. Williamson: Copyright © 1992 by Marianne Williamson. Reprinted by permission of HarperCollins Publishers, Inc. **115**, Reprinted with special permission of King Features Syndicate. **129**, Battista: reprinted by permission. **141**, Barry: reprinted with permission of *Tropic* magazine. **148**, May: reprinted by permission of Cartoon Features Syndicate. **149**, Friedman: reprinted by permission. Navasky: Copyright © 1992 by The New York Times Company. Reprinted by permission. **168**, Tupy: reprinted with permission of Jack Rosenbaum. **175**, Ink Inc.: reprinted by permission; Tammeus: reprinted by permission of *The Kansas City Star*. **176**, Douglas: Copyright © 1992 by The New York Times Company. Reprinted by permission. **180**, "Graffiti" reprinted by permission of United Feature Syndicate, Inc. **197**, Rich: Copyright © 1981 by The New York Times Company. Reprinted by permission. **208**, van der Post: reprinted by permission of William Morrow & Co., Inc. **212**, Battista: reprinted by permission. **213**, Crosby: reprinted with permission of the Jeff Davis County *Ledger*.